D1715587

Intensive Behavior Therapy
(PGPS-112)

Pergamon Titles of Related Interest

Anchin/Kiesler HANDBOOK OF INTERPERSONAL
PSYCHOTHERAPY
Brenner THE EFFECTIVE PSYCHOTHERAPIST: Conclusions from
Practice and Research
Hersen/Bellack BEHAVIORAL ASSESSMENT: A Practical
Handbook, Second Edition
Karoly/Kanfer SELF-MANAGEMENT AND BEHAVIOR CHANGE:
From Theory to Practice
Walker CLINICAL PRACTICE OF PSYCHOLOGY: A Guide for
Mental Health Professionals
Wolpe THE PRACTICE OF BEHAVIOR THERAPY, Third Edition

Related Journals*

ADVANCES IN BEHAVIOUR RESEARCH AND THERAPY
BEHAVIOUR RESEARCH AND THERAPY
CLINICAL PSYCHOLOGY REVIEW
JOURNAL OF BEHAVIOR THERAPY AND EXPERIMENTAL
PSYCHIATRY
PERSONALITY AND INDIVIDUAL DIFFERENCES

*Free specimen copies available upon request.

PERGAMON GENERAL PSYCHOLOGY SERIES
EDITORS
Arnold P. Goldstein, *Syracuse University*
Leonard Krasner, *SUNY at Stony Brook*

Intensive Behavior Therapy
The Behavioral Treatment of
Complex Emotional Disorders

John C. Papajohn
Brandeis University

PERGAMON PRESS
New York • Oxford • Toronto • Sydney • Paris • Frankfurt

Pergamon Press Offices:

U.S.A. Pergamon Press Inc., Maxwell House, Fairview Park, Elmsford, New York 10523, U.S.A.

U.K. Pergamon Press Ltd., Headington Hill Hall, Oxford OX3 0BW, England

CANADA Pergamon Press Canada Ltd., Suite 104, 150 Consumers Road, Willowdale, Ontario M2J 1P9, Canada

AUSTRALIA Pergamon Press (Aust.) Pty. Ltd., P.O. Box 544, Potts Point, NSW 2011, Australia

FRANCE Pergamon Press SARL, 24 rue des Ecoles, 75240 Paris, Cedex 05, France

FEDERAL REPUBLIC OF GERMANY Pergamon Press GmbH, Hammerweg 6, 6242 Kronberg/Taunus, Federal Republic of Germany

Library of Congress Cataloging in Publication Data

Papajohn, John.

Intensive behavior therapy.

(Pergamon general psychology series ; 112)
Bibliography: p.
Includes index.
1. Behavior therapy. 2. Behavior therapy--Case studies. I. Title. II. Series. [DNLM: 1. Affective disorders--Therapy. 2. Behavior therapy. WM 425 P213i]
RC489.B4P36   1982   616.89'142   82-5425
ISBN 0-08-025544-2   AACR2

Printed in the United States of America

To My Wife Eudokia
Who Made It Possible

Contents

Preface

In an informal meeting with Boston area behavior therapists in the early 1970s, Skinner talked about the rich opportunities that he could see ahead for the application of learning principles in a broad range of human endeavors. He mentioned, in this context, ecology, political science, and other related disciplines and then, almost as an afterthought, the area of mental illness. In a kind of reflective tone, as I processed it, he lamented that he hadn't paid more attention to psychotherapy as an important focus of behaviorism. I shared his lament.

An enormous amount of research has indeed been done by many in this area since that time. Only recently, however, have behaviorists been willing to focus on "traditional" psychotherapeutic approaches as a legitimate area of study. The effort until now has been to underscore the theoretical and methodological differences that separate behaviorism from psychoanalysis. It is now time for us to consider the commonalities that connect us. This book was conceived as a step in this direction. Its beginnings derive from the first undergraduate course I took in psychology at Columbia University with Fred Keller. The course, "Principles of Psychology," was my second choice since the parallel offering in General Psychology was oversubscribed. I was lucky that it was. This initiation into psychology was an enriching experience that was to remain with me throughout my career. It did not seem so to me then.

After completing a Master's Degree in experimental psychology in the graduate school at Columbia, I was impatient to "get on with it" and immersed myself in psychoanalytic theory as a graduate student in clinical psychology at Boston University. It was there that I learned to be a clinician. Intensive experience with careful supervision prepared me to respect the complexities of the clinical therapeutic process with a broad range of disturbances in many patients. My supervisors were psychoanalysts who patiently shepherded me through the difficult and anxiety laden experiences of learning how to listen, to support, and to interpret. I was too excited about these experiences of gradual unfolding of my clinical understanding to question the theoretical position of those who were giving me so much.

This came later when, as a staff psychotherapist, I was supervised by Eugenia Haufman at Brandeis University in the student counseling service. She quickly registered her impatience with my nondirective stance. She introduced me to the insights of Andras Angyal (*Neurosis and Treatment: A Holistic Theory,* by Andras Angyal, edited by E. Haufman & R. M. Jones; John Wiley & Sons, New York, 1965). This was a pivotal developmental experience for me because it taught me to question extant theory and to explore alternative ways of looking at what I was experiencing in the therapeutic situation. Her insights and those of Angyal's provided me with a topographic description of the neurotic process that broadened immeasurably my understanding of what it was all about—far beyond any learning I had yet acquired. This happened in the early 1960s concurrent with my research work with John Spiegel in the Department of Social Relations at Harvard on acculturation stress in members of American ethnic groups.

I became exposed to Joseph Wolpe's work a bit later, in the mid-sixties. I knew about his laboratory work with animal subjects in South Africa while I was still at Columbia, but I couldn't see its application to human neuroses. It seemed too far removed from psychotherapy as I then understood it. Now the significance of what he was describing became evident to me. I was by now seasoned sufficiently as a therapist and equipped theoretically in the principles of behaviorism to see the potential of "behavior therapy." The therapeutic possibilities of this approach excited me. I attended Wolpe's summer workshop in behavior therapy at the Eastern Pennsylvania Psychiatric Institute in 1969.

I immediately began to apply what I had learned in the treatment of my patients. At this juncture, I saw private adult patients, who represented a broad spectrum of neurotic difficulties, for more than twenty hours a week. From the onset I did not limit my behavioral treatment to selected patients with circumscribed symptoms, such as phobias and compulsions. I saw the broader implications of Pavlovian and Skinnerian theory for the treatment of disordered emotions in a variety of patients with different presenting problems. Actually, Wolpe taught me this. The transition from the traditional psychodynamic model to the behavioral one was not, however, an easy and smooth process. I experienced the ambivalence and confusion of an immigrant adapting to a new culture. I experienced, in other words, a high level of "cognitive dissonance." I tried to reduce this at times by rejecting outright those insights into the clinical process that derived from psychoanalytic theory. I was determined to do a careful "behavioral analysis"—"target" the behavior that needed modification and then apply the appropriate behavioral techniques. Of course this didn't work. Confronted with the ineffectiveness of this simplistic posture, I would then reject the whole behavioral approach as ill conceived and irrelevant. Also my understanding of sociocultural determinants of behavior which derived from my work on American ethnic groups was not even considered as relevant.

Gradually, over many trials and much error, the "integration" described in this book emerged. It has to be underscored that this "integration" has occurred at a clinical, not at a conceptual or theoretical, level. It involves looking at what "is" from a behavioral perspective and not excluding those phenomena that were first described to us by Freud. Freud also interpreted those phenomena. We need not subscribe to these interpretations if those that derive from learning theory can better "order the data."

Joseph Cautela supervised my early fledgling attempts to do behavior therapy. Chester Bennett, the Chairman of the Clinical Psychology Department at Boston University, offered me the opportunity to study there. I am grateful to him. William A. Hire, my professor in that department, supported me at a time when I needed it. Aaron Lazare of the Massachusetts General Hospital Department of Psychiatry encouraged me to prepare earlier versions of the introductory chapters of this book for *Outpatient Psychiatry, Diagnosis and Treatment* which he edited (Williams & Wilkins, 1979). John Spiegel, a psychoanalyst who has been my associate for the last twenty years, taught me through his "Transactional Systems Theory" to be aware of that complexly interrelated universe of events that determine how we behave.

My wife, Eudokia, an experienced psychotherapist, served as my ready "consultant" in unraveling those subtle "dynamics" of the more difficult patients I was treating.

Pearl Robinson, who typed the manuscript, went beyond her obligation to do a competent typing job by pointing out inconsistencies in the text.

Jerome Frank, my editor at Pergamon Press, has been unusually patient and supportive throughout this effort to produce a final manuscript. I am grateful to him.

Arnold Goldstein of Syracuse University, a consulting editor for Pergamon Press, first expressed interest in this project. His support helped to sustain my hope that it could be a worthwhile endeavor.

Introduction

This book was written for clinicians who are interested in exploring a new modality for the treatment of complex neurotic disorders. The behavior therapy movement has opened up exciting new vistas in the understanding of emotional suffering in humans that have provided methods for effecting therapeutic change in conditions which have proven refractory to change by other psychological therapies. Furthermore, behavior therapy has produced dramatic changes in a relatively small number of sessions in disorders that have consumed the energies of therapist and patient for inordinately protracted periods of time in the past. These facts, however, have had little impact on the traditionally trained therapist for whom this approach has never been considered seriously as a viable alternative to the methods in which they were trained. Their reasons for this have often been reasonable and carefully considered determinations based, in part, on their reading of the behavior therapy literature. This model, they have concluded, does not deal with the complexity of the therapeutic process as they have experienced it over years of practice. They are impatient with simple solutions to complex problems. The prospect of focusing on an individual's compulsive thinking or aberrant sexual behavior or phobia without treating the "whole person" leaves them feeling uneasy and impatient at the naiveté at best or, at worst, the irresponsibility that sometimes characterizes this approach. Experienced clinicians know better than to talk and act that way.

Behavior therapists themselves have done little to dispel these misconceptions of what goes on in the therapeutic interaction in behavior therapy. Journal articles consistently limit their reports to succinct descriptions of techniques applied and outcomes obtained. The human interactions in the patient-therapist relationship are left out. Readers conclude that the therapeutic process (if one can call it that) is a mechanical one devoid of human feeling, care, and commitment. The characterization of behavior modification as a "mind controlling" set of conditioning techniques with potential for violating human dignity depicted in the public media has not served to counteract this perception. The misuse of what is purported to be behavior modification in prisons and other institutional settings has also served to consolidate the image of behavioral treatment as an arena the well-trained and committed therapist best avoid.

Some psychodynamically trained clinicians somehow manage to overcome these barriers by considering behavior therapy as a viable treatment modality (Wachtel, 1977). They are willing to explore the possibility of its use in the treatment of discrete symptoms such as phobias, overweight, and others. The real work of therapy, however, remains for them a psychodynamic process where insight provides the modes of basic (intrapsychic) change. Behavior therapy might also be considered as the treatment of last resort when all else has failed—especially when an intractable symptom constitutes a central feature of the patient's syndrome.

The experienced behavior therapist approaches the treatment of a patient from an entirely different set of assumptions. He/she assumes that a symptom may not indeed be an isolated instance of disordered behavior in an otherwise well-functioning individual. In the initial behavioral analysis stage of the treatment, he/she explores intensively the relationship of the presenting problem, or symptoms, to the total psychological functioning of the individual. The treatment plan that is developed is based on this broad understanding and includes a multiple set of behavior change operations. The therapeutic alliance is considered a critical aspect of the treatment process and great care is invested in consolidating it. The implementation of a treatment strategy rarely proceeds in a straightforward manner with the sequential application of different techniques. Those phenomena described and labeled in psychoanalytic theory as "resistance," "transference," "defense," and others do not cease to exist when a behavioral therapeutic posture is taken in the approach to the treatment of neurotic disorders. They are indeed identified and dealt with within a behavioral frame of reference; however, they are conceptualized quite differently and managed differently. This is what this book is about. The major objective is to present the reader with an in-depth, multidimensional picture of the therapeutic process itself. The case histories constitute essentially a process analysis of the therapist-patient interaction in the therapy room. A detailed description is first provided of the various parameters of that interaction. These include basic issues such as theoretical assumptions that undergird the therapist's ordering of the clinical process, the establishment of the therapeutic alliance, the diagnostic or behavioral analysis phase of treatment, the development of a treatment strategy and the management of classical issues such as avoidance behaviors (resistance) and generalization (transference). The complex interplay of these parameters in the patient-therapist interaction process is presented in a manner that attempts to clarify areas of commonality as well as those distinct differences between behavior therapy and other more classical, i.e., psychodynamically based, systems. A major difference that needs to be noted here is that in behavior therapy, major therapeutic change is expected to occur outside the interview room in the management of stressful interpersonal and other events in his daily life. The interrelationship of changes in concrete behavior to changes in thinking and feeling processes will be especially concentrated on.

Chapter 1, Theoretical Foundation of Behavior Therapy, provides a brief overview of the theoretical assumptions undergirding behavior therapy. It sketches the main outlines of Pavlovian and Skinnerian learning theory for those readers who have had little or no previous orientation to this area.

Chapter 2, The Behavioral Analysis, describes the diagnostic process in which a therapeutic alliance is made during the initial history taking and data collection phase of the treatment. Special care is taken here to differentiate the functional analysis of the disordered behavior (the identification of the immediate causal events that precede and the consequences that follow it) from the traditional mental status examination where a diagnostic label is placed on the patient. The different steps included in the design of the treatment strategy are also included in this chapter. The work done during the therapeutic hour through which maladaptive behaviors are unlearned and the adaptive behaviors acquired (the replicative functions) will be related to the work initiated by the therapist (the instigative functions) and carried out by the patient outside the interview room.

An overview of the techniques that are employed by behavior therapists is provided in Chapter 3, Behavioral Techniques. While not intended to be exhaustive, this chapter will acquaint the reader with some of the representative techniques and the rationale underlying their use.

Chapter 4, Clinical Issues, will be of special interest to the psychodynamically trained therapist. A behavioral formulation of those classical phenomena known to all therapists (that is, transference, resistance, and others) is provided and their management in the behavioral therapeutic process described.

The four case histories comprising Chapters 5 through 8 were selected to provide examples of the treatment of complex neurotic disorders with different presenting problems; that is, a classical agoraphobia, an obsessional rumination disorder, a contamination phobia, and a case of "free floating" nonspecific anxiety. It is in these chapters that a detailed account is given of the interactions between therapist and patient during the various stages of treatment defined above. The process is analyzed with the nonbehaviorally-oriented therapist in mind.

The above description of the presenting problems of the four individuals that were treated does not correspond completely to the diagnostic categories elaborated in the third edition of *The Diagnostic and Statistical Manual of Mental Disorders* published by the American Psychiatric Association (*D.S.M.* III, 1981). This is consistent with the theoretical underpinnings of the behavioral analysis that differentiates it from the more traditional differential diagnosis. This point is detailed in Chapter 2, The Behavioral Analysis and the Design of the Treatment Strategy. The diagnostic criteria for agoraphobia in *D.S.M.* III (p. 227) are consistent with those that describe the individual with "a classical agoraphobia." Both "obsessional rumination disorder" and "contamination phobia" are subsumed under the diagnostic criteria for Obsessive Compulsive Disorder (*D.S.M.* III, p. 235); "free floating" anxiety corresponds to Generalized Anxiety Disorder (*D.S.M.* III, p. 233).

1

Theoretical Foundations of

Behavior Therapy

In behavior therapy, disorders of thinking, feeling, and acting are conceptualized as maladaptive responses to environmental events that have been learned by the patient in the past and are maintained in the present by their reinforcing consequences. The principles operating in the acquisition and maintenance of these behaviors are to be found in the modern learning theories of Pavlov and Skinner. While affective, cognitive and conative (overt response) patterns are interactive processes, it is important to separate them conceptually for purposes of diagnosis, as well as for the subsequent design of treatment strategies focused selectively on each of them.

The etiology of affective disorders such as anxiety, depression, and hostility is located in an individual's maladaptive interaction with the environment. The anxiety response is stimulated in different situations that are not in themselves intrinsically dangerous, but that have acquired noxious properties through past learning. Phobias are examples of learned anxiety reactions to specific situations, while generalized anxiety may be experienced in a broad range of everyday situations resulting in more pervasive inhibition of adaptive behaviors.

In cases where depression is the primary presenting problem, the therapist assumes, in the absence of organic etiological factors, that the patient is ineffective in obtaining the necessary emotional satisfactions and other reinforcements in his daily life. He either lacks the appropriate repertoire of behavior for obtaining reinforcements or his available repertoire is no longer appropriate to new conditions in which he finds himself/herself. The sudden loss of a loved one, changing one's occupational status, and moving chronologically into a different stage of life are examples of radical shifts in behavior which necessitate corollory shifts in behavior for effective interactions.

Chronic states of generalized hostility that impair smooth interpersonal functioning are conceptualized as learned maladaptive anger responses. They can be stimulated by current situations where the individual lacks the appropriate repertoire to respond effectively to frustrating circumstances. Anger responses are maintained when they are reinforced through desired changes in the behavior of those toward whom they are directed.

Disorders of cognition are viewed as maladaptive thinking habits which constitute the "set" or covert verbal labeling process through which the individual experiences the "meaning" of external and internal events. These mediational processes can take the form of irrational beliefs; that is, attitudes and expectations that were learned in the past and result in ineffective functioning in interpersonal and other situations in the present. These cognitive habits include irrational assumptions of which the patient may be fully aware, as well as assumptions that he may not be aware of at all. An example of the latter are attitudes about sex based on misinformation or the distortion of information acquired in the past. An example of the former is the attitude that one must be liked by everyone one interacts with in order to be a worthwhile individual. A common example of a cognitive disturbance is the reaction, "I must be insane," that follows the subjective experience of high levels of anxiety in a patient. The anxiety initially caused by an external event is potentiated by this verbal labeling process.

Obsessive ruminations are categorized under maladaptive cognitive habits. While at first they may be a reaction to anxiety-evoking environmental conditions, they come to assume the function of noxious stimuli that in turn activate further anxiety, thus forming a spiraling chain of repetitive cognitive events resulting in increasingly higher levels of anxiety. Paranoid states like obsessional symptoms are examples of severe cognitive distortion which are learned in reaction to high levels of anxiety over an extended period of time.

Disorders of conation can take the form of specific symptoms involving skeletal-motor responses that disrupt effective interaction with the environment. Certain "normal" actions cannot be successfully executed or, conversely, individuals are unable to stop themselves from engaging in certain undesirable acts. Sexual dysfunctioning is a prime example of the former. Compulsive behaviors (such as tics, checking rituals, decontamination behaviors, as well as fetishes, voyeurism, and others) are examples of the latter. It is clear that most of these maladaptive behaviors serve the function of reducing anxiety in the patient. However, reducing the antecedent anxiety is not always the sufficient condition for eliminating the symptom. When it is conceptualized as learned motor behavior, its elimination can be planned in accordance with deconditioning principles.

Hysterical conversion symptoms and other "psychosomatic" disorders are examples of conative disorders which are conceptualized as learned behavior.

It becomes evident from the above overview that behavior therapy is based on a conceptual model that lends itself to the understanding of a broad range of disordered behaviors and is not limited to techniques employed in the elimination of discrete symptoms. It becomes important, therefore, to elaborate the conceptual model undergirding this therapeutic modality in order that the strategies, methods and techniques that emanate from it can be better understood.

Behavior therapy is based on the philosophical assumption that the organism and the environment are an interacting system of events; the organism reacting from birth to external conditions in both the physical and the social environment is changed by those conditions in predictable ways (Krasner, 1969, pp. 537–569). On the basis of this experience with the external world, the organism acquires consistent patterns of reacting to new conditions as he traverses the life cycle. In this formulation, the mind cannot be separated conceptually from the responding organism. The behavior of the responding organism, modified by previous experience, becomes the subject matter of psychology, the study of the mind. The use of the word organism here implies, of course, that man shares with lower species a common biological heritage and, furthermore, that it is in the biological-environmental interaction that explanations of the nature of behavior of all species need to be pursued.

The method of inquiry deriving from this philosophical posture is familiar to all natural scientists. The scientific method is based on the principle that only objectively observable and objectively verifiable data can be included in a science of human behavior. Biological environmental interactions, furthermore, should be quantifiable. The natural course of inquiry into the meaning of the behavior of organisms involves the observance of the rules of the scientific method. These include the formulation of a theory about the cause-effect relationship between biological and environmental events from which hypotheses are derived that lend themselves to experimental verification through empirical testing.

This is the course that the two major contributors to a science of human behavior have taken: Ivan Pavlov (1941) and B. F. Skinner (1953). Their theories of respondent and operant conditioning, respectively, are based on the principle of associationism initially formulated by Aristotle (who, incidentally, was both the disciple of Plato and the creator of the scientific method on which most of modern science is based). Aristotle first elaborated on the position that the organism and the environment are an interacting system of events, that connections of associations are bonded in this interaction, and that these associations (located by him in the heart) constitute the reservoir of experiences which form the basis on which future environmental events are responded to. For Aristotle, the soul or the mind of an individual organism was its function, i.e., its behavior, which was not separable from its body. When Aristotle talked about behavior, he was not referring to motor behavior only but to thinking and to feeling as well (Murphy, 1949).

Pavlov's early experiments are too well-known to have to be described here at any length (1927). He demonstrated that an associative bond or connection (that is, a conditioned response) could be effected by pairing a stimulus such as food, which naturally evoked an automatic response, salivation, with a stimulus such as the sounding of a bell that in the natural world did not elicit this reaction. The sound of the bell and the salivation response constituted a new stimulus-response connection, a new conditioned behavior.

Pavlov and his associates conducted a broad research program in which the properties of the conditioned reflex, as they labeled it, were explored. The principles of generalization and discrimination that they elaborated on concern us here. Generalization refers to the phenomenon whereby a stimulus similar in its properties to the conditioned one (such as the sound of a bell of higher pitch than the one originally paired with the food) elicits the same salivary response as did the original lower pitched tone. Discrimination refers to that phenomenon in which a stimulus is sufficiently different in its properties from the conditioned one (a sound of a bell of such high pitch that the organism separates it from the tone originally paired with food) so that it does not elicit the salivary response as did the original tone of a lower pitch.

Skinner demonstrated that not only reactive respondent, autonomic responses could be conditioned, but that skeletal behavior with which an organism actively interacted or operated on the environment also could be modified by arranging for that behavior to be followed by reinforcing consequences. When a motor response, such as bar pressing by a rat in a box, was followed by food an associative connection between the visual stimuli of the bar and the pressing response was bonded. This is to say that the probability of the rat's pressing the bar was markedly increased when a rewarding consequence or "reinforcement" was arranged to follow it. Skinner discovered through years of laboratory research with animals that the schedule by which reinforcements were administered (whether a response was followed by food each time it was emitted, or at a fixed ratio of reinforced to nonreinforced responses, or at an irregular time interval) determined the strength of the responses that they followed, that is, the rate and the amount of energy that the animal would expend in maintaining the acquired behavior. His measure of the strength of a conditioned response was extinction, or the number of times the animal would continue to press the bar when reinforcement was withheld and reward no longer was contingent on the emission of this response.

The theoretical principles formulated by Pavlov and Skinner have been applied in the conceptualization and treatment of a broad variety of neurotic as well as psychotic disorders. Both respondent and operant tracks are followed in the analysis and treatment of a disorder of feeling, thinking, and acting. The respondent approach has been elaborated by Wolpe, who introduced behavior therapy to American psychiatry in 1954 in a paper entitled "Reciprocal Inhibition as the Main Basis of Psychotherapeutic Effects" (Wolpe, 1954). He described a method for the elimination of maladaptive anxiety reactions in humans based on laboratory experiments with cats. In these experiments he produced "experimental neurosis" in cats by confining them to a cage and administering high-voltage, low-amperage shocks. The animal, shocked in this manner, became conditioned to responding with severe anxiety reactions not only when again placed in the cage, but also to places resembling the physical properties of the experimental situation. The animal's anxiety reactions had generalized, in the Pavlovian definition of that term, to stimulus conditions similar to those in which the anxiety reactions had first been associated or learned. The further the cat was taken from the experimental cage, the less its manifest anxiety became. This was hypothesized to occur because the animal was now able to discriminate, again, in the Pavlovian sense, dissimilar, non-noxious stimuli, from those associated with the onset of the shock in the cage. The unlearning, or counterconditioning, of the animal's neurotic anxiety was designed in accordance with the principle of reciprocal inhibition first formulated by Sherrington (Wolpe, 1958). The anxiety response to a noxious stimulus can be eliminated in accordance with this principle if the following conditions are made to occur: (1) A substitute, competing response to anxiety is arranged to occur when the organism is exposed to the noxious stimuli; (2) The organism is exposed to stimuli eliciting low levels of anxiety while the competing, substitute counter-anxiety response is arranged to occur at relatively higher levels of intensity. Wolpe used the feeding response to inhibit the anxiety reaction of the experimentally conditioned cat. The animal was placed at a far enough distance from the experimental cage for only a low level of anxiety to be elicited. Simultaneously, the animal was induced to eat food. The pleasurable eating sensations, stronger than the weak anxiety responses, gradually weakened them further until the animal could eat comfortably with no manifest anxiety. In a graded step-wise fashion, over several days, the animal was moved closer to the experimental cage until it was able to feed in the place where it had been originally shocked. The stimulus-response between the noxious stimulus conditions (the cage) and the response (anxiety) were broken. The animal unlearned, so to speak, to be afraid; it was counterconditioned, or therapized. The behavioral technique called systematic desensitization developed by Wolpe (1958) for the deconditioning of anxiety reactions is based on the principle of reciprocal inhibition. I will describe this technique in some detail later.

From a respondent conditioning point of view, human neuroses are learned anxiety reactions of a complex nature acquired by the patient, often during childhood, through exposure to conditions of high emotional arousal. The conditions of high anxiety arousal are usually experienced by the child in interactions with significant adults. A typical such condition is overcontrol, where the parent inhibits the free movement of the child. This can cause rage responses that are followed by punishment, resulting in subjectively felt anxiety. A consequence of this chain of events can be inhibition—the child ceases to resist the controlling parent and experiences instead anxiety of an anticipatory nature. He/she has learned that movement toward gratification of needs is followed by frustration and punishment. In subsequent interactions with the environment, anticipatory anxiety becomes a discriminative cue or signal of impending punishment, which may result in the individual avoiding entirely situations where the potential gratification of needs could result in a dangerous consequence.

It can be seen that this explanatory concept for what is termed "repression" in psychoanalytic theory is based on associationist rather than developmental assumptions. It is in the organism-environment interaction that behavior is modified. The child discriminates which conditions result in punishment; he anticipates the outcome and this anticipation leads to maneuvers to avoid the feared consequence. Through the process of generalization, a broad range of conditions similar to the ones in which the individual learned to experience anxiety as a child now elicit similar emotional reactions in his/her adult life. He cannot get on with his boss, i.e., generalization of negative feelings toward an authoritarian father; he/she is uncomfortable with women and the prospect of sexual relations make him anxious. His sexual feelings were associated with "guilt" or the anticipation of punishment since he/she learned in his home environment that sex was sinful and could not be discussed.

Specific symptoms such as phobias and compulsions are conceptualized as anxiety response habits. These symptoms are learned responses to anxiety-evoking conditions. They serve the function of reducing anxiety reactions. High places (acrophobia) are stimuli that have become associated with the fear of falling, which in turn is associated with fear of losing control or, in extreme conditions, fear of dying. The avoidance, or escape, from high buildings eliminates this fear. The performance of compulsive rituals such as checking results in immediate relief from anxiety caused by situations in the past where, for example, the individual became anxious because of angry feelings which he feared could get out of control unless they were checked.

Skinner's (1956) operant conditioning principles have been employed for the modification of behavior in a variety of situations, and with a variety of populations ranging from normal children in the classroom to psychotic individuals on a psychiatric ward. The assumption undergirding the various therapeutic approaches or behavior change strategies in these diverse populations are the same, i.e., effective functioning in the areas of feeling, thinking, and acting is contingent on the individual's effective procurement of the necessary gratifications for living in his/her interaction with the interpersonal environment. The conceptualization of depressive affective states will serve to illustrate this approach in a particular clinical condition (Ferster, 1973, pp. 857–870). Extreme emotional deprivation in early childhood predisposes the individual for a low rate of active responding to opportunities in the current interpersonal environment for the gratification of emotional needs. The individual may never have learned how and when to act effectively in order to get others to respond to him. He/she lacks the essential repertoire for connecting with others in the complex interpersonal environment; he/she withdraws because he/she doesn't know what to do and because what he/she has attempted to do has not resulted in the expected consequence. When this happens in the sexual area, we find that shy and inhibited individuals never learned appropriate ways of approaching and responding to a potential sexual partner. Widowed and divorced people often find they must learn new ways of meeting their emotional needs, which requires a radical shift in patterned response habits. In the case of a widowed individual the "working through" of grief may be the necessary, but not sufficient, condition for an adequate adjustment to a new life situation. It may also require learning new ways to obtain reinforcements subsumed under the general heading of "emotional." Much of what is called ennui in middlessence lends itself to an operant interpretation. Old patterns for getting pleasure or enjoyment may no longer be available when one has reached an age designated as the one when one is no longer "young." Maturing essentially involves determining what lifestyle changes need to be effected in order to secure a new and continuing source of gratification in one's life.

It is to the individual's interaction with his interpersonal environment in the present that one looks to determine whether basic needs are met. The absence of sources of continuing and effective reinforcers is seen as causally related to disordered affective states such as anger and depression. The individual may be ineffective for whatever reason in obtaining reinforcements, but it is in the present where change can take place by helping him/her to restructure his interactions for more successful outcomes.

2
The Behavioral Analysis and the Design
of the Treatment Strategy

The standard questions of the traditional mental status examination provide information that is of limited value to the behavioral clinician since they do not provide for a description of those organism-environment interactions that constitute a functional analysis of the patient's behavior (Ferster, 1965). Topographic designations, i.e., the categorization of disordered behavior through the use of diagnostic labels, provides the clinician with only a still photograph. Inferences must be drawn as to what went before; what caused the described behavior; and what its consequences are on the interpersonal environment, that is, how it affected others. The predictive value of these diagnostic categories varies markedly between patients. While their heuristic value cannot be overlooked, since they were developed from observations of the actual behavior of patients, the behavioral clinician prefers to rely instead on obtaining information about the specific conditions under which the disordered behavior occurs in a particular patient.

In the initial diagnostic or behavioral analysis stage of treatment, the therapist is guided by the theoretical assumptions and learning principles elaborated earlier. In taking a history, he/she is concerned with those anamneses of the patient which provide information about those significant experiences in his life including relationships with parents, siblings, and sexual education, that have conditioned him to act or react in his current environment in predictable ways. It is the current environment, however, that is the major focus of the behavioral analysis. Here the clinician seeks to determine what the *independent* variables are; that is, the events in the daily life of the patient that are causally related to the occurrences of the disordered thinking, feeling, or acting—behaviors that are the target for therapeutic change. The second aspect of this functional analysis is the identification of

8

the *dependent* variables accompanying the target behaviors. This refers to the quality and quantity of the reinforcing consequences of the behavior, or what changes are produced in the behavior of those with whom the patient is interacting. How significant others react to the anxiety, disturbed thinking, or inappropriate behavior of the patient determines the frequency with which that behavior will continue to occur when the same or similar causal condition or situational variables are present (Kanfer & Saslow, 1969a, 1969b).

THE PATIENT-THERAPIST INTERACTION

Before detailing the various dimensions of the process of behavioral analysis, it is important to describe the patient-therapist interaction. From the first contact, the behaviorally oriented therapist is concerned with two major interrelated aspects of the therapeutic confrontation. In the first instance he/she is concerned with developing a therapeutic alliance with his/her patient. Secondly, his objective is to share his/her conceptual model with the patient.

The patient is not related to as a "conditioned organism." He/she is related to as an individual with difficulties caused primarily by faulty learning or maladaptive experiences from the past and are maintained in the present by specific definable conditions. The therapist is empathetic and supportive. He/she knows that the therapeutic outcome will be determined in part by the degree he/she is able to relate effectively to his patient. To this end, he selectively reinforces the patient for those strengths that become evident during this assessment "phase" of the treatment. Past achievements and current areas where functioning is effective are responded to with appropriate comments. In the interaction itself he attempts to enhance feelings of effectiveness and self-worth in the patient. He/she, therefore, does not respond to self-deprecatory statements or statements of helplessness when these are designed to elicit a reassuring response in the therapist. Obsessive preoccupations containing self-deprecatory themes, for example, are selectively not responded to, since to do so increases the frequency of their occurrence. The reassurance the patient seeks has only a transient positive effect and, in fact, in the long run the relief they provide can serve to reinforce or increase the subjectively experienced discomfort, whether it be anxiety or another maladaptive emotional response. Escape from pain (avoidance behavior) is often mistakenly reinforced by what is commonly identified as "empathy" or support. The experienced clinician is able to provide support when it is appropriate and does so freely and spontaneously. However, he/she does not passively permit himself/herself to be shaped by the patient into reinforcing avoidance-maintaining maneuvers through empathetic responses.

The second guiding principle that orients the behavior therapist in the initial diagnostic phase of treatment is what can be termed the "reculturization" process. The patient is oriented to structuring his problem in behavioral terms which are not the common mode for labeling human experiences in western culture (Krasner, 1969, pp. 537–569). The therapist shares his/her theoretical assumptions about disorders of thinking, feeling, and acting with the patient. He/she mediates the major premise, i.e., that his/her suffering is caused by maladaptive behaviors learned in the past and maintained in the present by identifiable conditions. In the well-educated patient this is accomplished directly through conceptual inputs when the opportunity occurs naturally. It is also mediated indirectly through the particular form of questioning in the history-taking when inquiries are made into the current functioning of the patient. He/she poses his questions in cause and effect (stimuli and response) terms. The therapist searches with the patient for precipitating conditions in the past where the disordered thinking, feeling, and acting may have been learned. He/she then explores in detail current life situations, and explores how the disorder continues to be maintained in the present; that is, what the payoff or reinforcing consequences are (Wolpe, 1973, chap. 3). This method of inquiry essentially equips the patient to become a trained scientific observer of his own behavior, and helps develop the common basis for his therapeutic interactions with the therapist throughout the course of therapy.

In neurotic patients who have become concerned about their mental health because of experiencing high levels of anxiety and confusion in their thinking and who may be preoccupied with "going crazy," the internalization of the behavioral assumptions often results in a reduction of their irrational fears. It becomes possible to impose a logical structure on their feelings that, by definition, reduces their anxiety.

It has become evident from the above description that the behavior therapist is active and directive in his interaction with the patient. It will become even clearer in the rest of this chapter that the therapist focuses the clinical inquiry in the behavioral analysis on the predetermined areas of functioning.

However, this approach is not to be confused with a rigid, authoritarian posture. It is in fact a collaborative effort in which the patient, sharing the conceptual model of the therapist, explores with him/her the origins of his difficulties. This point can become clearer if we consider the "role" of the behavior therapist as that of a third party intervener, the two parties at issue being that of the individual on the one hand and the relevant environment he interacts with on the other. The behavior therapist is contracted by the patient as an "expert consultant" in possession of technical skills to be employed in facilitating his/her disordered interactions with the environment. The major changes sought for are not expected to occur within the patient during the therapeutic session. They are designed to occur between the patient and his interpersonal environment outside the therapist's office in the actual milieu in which he functions. The therapist's objective is to assist the individual to learn alternative ways of functioning that can produce the satisfactions necessary for a rewarding life. The therapeutic setting does indeed provide the context for the unlearning or deconditioning of maladaptive cognitive, affective, and conative responses. The removal of a discrete symptom such as a compulsive motor response, or the deconditioning of a phobic response, may be accomplished in whole or in part in the therapist's office. The elimination of maladaptive behaviors, however, are not understood as goals in themselves. They are conceptualized, rather, as necessary steps toward the acquisition of alternative behaviors aimed toward broadening the range of effective interactions with the environment. The experience of a more satisfying and productive lifestyle is contingent on these changes.

The question of differential diagnosis needs to finally be broached before we detail the behavioral analysis state of treatment. In the course of the behavioral analysis the patient may manifest signs of a severe thought disorder or an affective disorder of psychotic proportions. The question must then be raised as to whether the patient is indeed an appropriate candidate for behavior therapy in an outpatient setting. Drug therapy may, indeed, be the indicated first choice of treatment; the question of psychological treatment may be postponed until the patient's condition has stabilized to the point where intervention of this kind can be effective.

TAKING A HISTORY: THE VERTICAL AND THE HORIZONTAL COURSE

In taking a history, both a vertical course is followed to the past life of the patient and a horizontal course to the more immediate events characterizing his/her present experience in a broad range of situations. The inquiry is also both specific and general in nature. The therapist employs the presenting problem or symptom as an organizing theme and inquires into its origins in the past. He explores the specific conditions under which the problem first appeared, what events preceded it, who were the significant individuals involved in its onset, and the consequences of the disordered behavior. What is important to determine here is what benefits, if any, are derived from the maintenance of symptoms or other disordered behavior. Often these "rewards" include support from significant others or the avoidance of anxiety through escape from aversive situations (negative reinforcement). In this manner, the course of the disorder is traced to the present when the therapist inquires into the current life of the patient in order to determine the events maintaining the maladaptive thinking, feeling, or acting behaviors. The precision with which this is done needs to be emphasized. The therapist is not satisfied with statements such as, "I am anxious all the time." Although the patient may feel this way, the objective facts are often quite at variance with this report. In response to questions from the therapist, the patient discovers that in fact he/she is anxious primarily in certain situations, and with certain people. Anxiety mounts to high levels, for example, when the individual prepares in the morning to go to a job where criticism and devaluation are expected from superiors or coworkers. Anxiety is further intensified in staff conferences where he/she is unable to assert himself/herself because of fear of reprisals from the authority figures who are present. As the end of the work day approaches, one's anxiety level decreases, is at a low level during free hours in the evening, and increases perceptibly again in the morning. Another hypothetical example can be the patient whose presenting problem is colitis. In response to direct questioning by the therapist, the patient reports that his/her colitis flares up as a consequence of feeling intense anger toward certain individuals whom he/she encounters in specific situations, such as on the job. A consequence of this intense somatic discomfort is that the individual leaves work and is ministered to by a spouse who is supportive and caring. The intensity of the somatic symptoms then decreases.

In cases where the patient has difficulty in identifying the conditions that are causally related to the onset of the disordered behavior, the therapist requests that in the interval between therapeutic sessions an hourly written log be kept of what he/she is doing and feeling in order that he/she become more sensitized to the stimulus conditions related to the problematic behavior.

It becomes important, also, to determine what corollary conditions may be causally related to the specific disordered behavior being explored. While it may be determined that anxiety is stimulated by identifiable environmental conditions (such as enclosed places, or being alone, or the controlling behavior of others), it can also be the case that stresses in another domain of experience may be affecting the patient's responses in those specific situations. For example, marital conflict that reduces the feeling of security in an individual can exacerbate a phobic reaction to specific stimuli to which it was originally conditioned, such as high or enclosed places. Anniversary of deaths, moving one's residence, changing one's job, getting married, reaching middle age, and other so-called existential crises constitute conditions that can affect the behavior disorder in question. This is not to say that the behavior disorder is viewed merely as a symptom of stresses whose causes are to be found elsewhere. The issue is conceptualized, rather, as one in which the individual is reacting with anxiety to situations other than those immediately related to the presenting problem. These corollary stress conditions sensitize and predispose the individual to respond to the anxiety-evoking stimuli in the immediate present with greater intensity than might otherwise be the case. The immediate situation which activates the individual's maladaptive thinking, feeling, or acting remains the major focus. However, the therapist may choose to attempt to alleviate stress in those identified corollary areas before the specific symptom or the disordered behavior is approached directly.

SOCIAL, CULTURAL AND BIOLOGICAL EVENTS

Having explored the origins of the presenting problem in the past and having identified the conditions of its occurrence and its consequences in the present, the therapist then moves to obtain a more general history. He/she is interested in understanding the patient's problem in the broader context of the social, cultural and biological conditions that characterize his/her life experience (Spiegel, 1971). Here, too, the focus is on both the past and the present; again both a vertical and horizontal course is followed in order to obtain information about significant events. The social and cultural conditions in which the individual grew up are investigated. Experiences with significant adults, siblings, and friends are reviewed and any traumatic events not necessarily connected to the presenting problem are explored. Childhood illnesses, as well as those during the crucial adolescent years, are reviewed. A careful sexual history is taken. The content areas, then, are similar to those concentrated on by psychodynamically oriented therapists. The focus, however, is on a precise identification of causal conditions and the consequences in the life of the patient of specific reactions to particular events or situations.

The current cultural, social, and biological conditions affecting the life of the patient are then explored following the horizontal course of inquiry. These conditions determine the nature of the day-to-day experiences the individual is exposed to in the present. Cultural prescriptions that vary in different regions of the country, as well as ethnic and subcultural variations, determine how the individual is expected to behave in specific situations (Papajohn & Spiegel, 1975). His social status is another important condition in this respect. Social class predetermines which behaviors are approved, and so selectively reinforced, in individuals comprising a particular position in the status hierarchy. The stresses, therefore, in the employment area, family area, and social area in general vary for the cultural and social characteristics of the individual's group.

The physical condition of the patient is also explored. In addition to possible organic etiological factors related to the presenting problem, the medical history of the patient provides the therapist with information related to a vital area of experience in his/her life. Current medical conditions can critically alter the individual's repertoire of available coping behavior.

An understanding of cultural, social, and biological conditions characterizing the past and current life of the patient is necessary for planning an effective intervention strategy. The immediate stimulus conditions activating the disordered behavior in a particular situation can better be identified if cultural, social, and biological factors are taken into account. The high anxiety arousal elicited by authority figures in the hypothetical example described earlier can more easily be identified by the therapist who has learned his/her patient was socialized in a very ideologically conservative ethnic family where submissive behavior toward parental figures was consistently reinforced. Assertive behavior toward people in power positions, therefore, elicits anxiety from the anticipation of punishment. However, the highly competitive work environment of this socially upward mobile individual demands just this assertiveness for effective functioning. He/she was socialized to function in an environment with basically different expectations of how to behave than the one he/she now finds himself/herself in. He/she has internalized cognitive expectancies at variance with those of employers and coworkers. The therapist, therefore, would approach the treatment of this patient differently than one whose anxiety in the presence of authority figures was conditioned in a family where the father was cruel and punishing toward the patient. While a direct deconditioning technique for anxiety (such as systematic desensitization) may be appropriate for the latter patient, it may not be for our hypothetical patient. Cognitive restructuring techniques may be more appropriate as the initial intervention procedure. This technique involves challenging at a cognitive level the patient's assumption that all authority figures expect those who relate to them to be submissive. In other words, the culturally patterned prescription about relationships to people in power positions needs to be dealt with through verbal cognitive inputs by the therapist, rather than by employing direct deconditioning procedures at the emotional level.

AREAS OF EFFECTIVE FUNCTIONING

The behavioral analysis is not limited only to the identification of maladaptive emotional, cognitive, and conative responses. It also focuses on determining the effective behavioral repertoire the patient has acquired in the past and is employing successfully in the present environment: the areas of life where the patient is able to interact in a manner that produces emotional satisfaction; work that he/she does successfully; friendships he/she has that are supportive and rewarding; special skills or abilities in the recreational sphere of activity. Other traits of the patient, such as intellectual ability and achievements, are noted by the therapist. This focus on identifying areas of effective functioning in the behavioral analysis stage is important for a series of reasons. First, they provide the therapist with ways of verbally reinforcing the patient when the opportunity presents itself. This can be crucial in patients whose attitudes about themselves are based on punitive experiences in which they have acquired cognitive habits of labeling what they do in negative terms. Second, areas where the patient is functioning effectively can be employed in the service of designing desired changes. An example would be the intellectually gifted individual who is passive in interpersonal relationships. The design of an assertive training program could employ situations where the patient's intellectual abilities could be brought to bear in learning effective interactions with others. On the other hand, some patients have learned effective ways of interacting with the environment, but for different reasons have ceased to employ them. These are individuals with a rich behavioral repertoire in areas of work or recreation, for example, who have narrowed their range of activities in a manner that produces progressively fewer gratifications. They have ceased to pursue interests that have high reinforcement value for them in both the work and recreational situations, and their range of satisfying social contacts is extremely limited. A careful hourly log of their week's activities reveals few reinforcing interactions. Patients are often amazed when they realize through this technique how they have allowed themselves to be shaped by external demands to a lifestyle characterized by a dearth of satisfying experiences (Lewinsohn, 1974; Lewinsohn & Graf, 1973, pp. 261–268; Lewinsohn & Libet, 1972, pp. 291–295). Sometimes ways learned in the past for obtaining satisfactions are no longer effective in the changed life conditions patients find themselves in as they move into a different life stage (middle age or retirement). Also, the loss of a spouse or other relied on sources of satisfying living can deprive the individual of long established patterns of effective interaction. The presenting problem in these cases may often be depression. A knowledge of what the patient is capable of doing by virtue of past learning can be extremely important in designing a therapeutic strategy to reverse the process.

BEHAVIORAL DEFICITS

Other individuals have never acquired the necessary repertoire for functioning effectively in their environment. Their problem is one of a deficit of appropriate behaviors, rather than disordered behavior. These deficits can occur in the area of thinking, feeling, or motor behavior.

In the cognitive area, while their intellectual ability may be adequate, they have acquired a narrow range of concepts for dealing with the complexities of life. These are the individuals who are often characterized as "naive." They have not learned how to realistically conceptualize what goes on in social situations. They make assumptions about others' behavior that is not warranted (such as, if one behaves fairly toward others, one can expect the same treatment in return), and so often fail in their efforts to be effective in interpersonal situations (Seligman, 1975).

In the affective realm an individual may not be able to react with appropriate feelings to different situations. The range of emotional responsiveness may be limited due to inhibition in the past. The patient becomes anxious when the appropriate emotional response is anger, or feels nothing at all when joy would be the appropriate feeling. Success became a discriminatory stimulus for anxiety since in the past getting what was desired was associated with punishment.

In the conative area a patient's difficulties may be due to a lack of requisite skills. Academic failures, for example, may not be due primarily to anxiety but to a lack of necessary study skills. Social failure may be due to the lack of such basic skills as driving a car, not knowing appropriate social graces, or not knowing where to go and how to meet the people with whom one wants to be. Too often the presence of inhibition clouds the fact that the patient never learned to do the things he/she wants to do. Anxiety may be a secondary reaction to lack of requisite skills in these instances rather than a primary causative factor.

QUESTIONNAIRES

In order to facilitate the data gathering in the behavioral analysis stage of treatment, the behavior therapist employs structured questionnaires through which information is obtained in the areas of functioning described above. They serve several of the goals of the behavioral analysis. First of all, the patient in filling them out is oriented to focusing on specific behaviors rather than the abstractions that might customarily be used to describe experiences. The schedules include a comprehensive range of samples of behavior that might be missed in the behavioral analysis interviews. They provide a baseline measure of disordered thinking, feeling, and acting from which the therapist can assess the actual changes that take place in the course of treatment. They also provide information on adaptive behaviors that can be employed by the therapist in designing therapeutic change strategies.

There are many questionnaires in use. A comprehensive description of these is provided by Cautela in *Behavior Analysis* (1977). The following are representative because they are used widely by behavior therapists and cover some of the basic areas of information described above.

The Life History Questionnaire (Lazarus, 1971) is comprehensive in scope. Its questions are designed to provide information on the general background of the patient as well as on specific problems. The areas include physical health; family, educational and occupational background; significant childhood experiences; sexual history; current problematic behaviors; attitudes toward self; past and present experiences with significant others; and interests, hobbies, and other activities. It also requires the patient to specify what expectations he/she has of the treatment.

The Fear Survey Schedule (Wolpe, 1973) is comprised of 106 items (experiences and stimuli) that the patient is asked to rate for the degree of anxiety they elicit. The items include situations such as high places or land, receiving injections, being criticized, and crowds. The variety of stimulus conditions is broad and the schedule designed to provide the therapist with a comprehensive range of specific stimuli that are fear-arousing in the patient.

Cautela's Reinforcement Schedule (Cautela & Kastenbaum, 1967) and Lewinsohn's Life Satisfaction Inventory (Lewinsohn & Libet, 1972) provide information on situations that are reinforcing for the patient. Lewinsohn's inventory provides information on the specific occasions when the patient experiences satisfactions in the course of his daily life, and also makes it possible to assess his satisfying experiences over the previous six months. Again the information provided is for specific situations, times, and places.

Personality inventories of a broad variety are employed by behavior therapists as standard procedures during the behavior analysis stage of treatment. Wolpe (1973) describes two of these: The Willoughby Personality Schedule and the Bernreuter S-S Scale. These instruments also make it possible to obtain samples of the patient's behavior before beginning treatment, as well as after the conclusion of treatment, in order that a more objective assessment of change can be made.

DESIGNING THE TREATMENT STRATEGY

The behavioral clinician reviews with the patient the results of the behavioral analysis. The next procedure involves designing behavior change strategies and determining the order of treatment of target behaviors identified in the behavior analysis stage. The latter is arrived at through a consideration of several complexly interrelated factors. A primary consideration is the degree to which the presenting problem has a disorganizing effect on the rest of the patient's life and so must be given top priority. Severe anxiety reactions, or specific symptoms such as compulsive checking or obsessive thinking, that do not allow the individual to carry on his daily work are cases in point. A second factor is the relative degree of difficulty that can be anticipated in changing a particular disordered behavior. When possible, behaviors that can be changed more easily are broached first since success with these will increase the probability that the patient will persevere with those that are more difficult. When the presenting problem is a specific symptom, such as a plane phobia or a compulsion, the decision must be made as to whether the elimination of the symptom will be attempted first or whether precedence should be given instead to corollary conditions not immediately related causally to the symptom. They could include, for example, fear of abandonment related to the anticipated termination of a marital relationship, or fear of loss of one's job, or anxiety that is instigated by rage felt toward a superior. The treatment of these conditions will often decrease the severity of the phobic reactions, but not necessarily eliminate the symptom. Both the immediate environmental stimulus conditions (i.e., buying a plane ticket, going to the airport, boarding the plane) must be dissociated from the anxiety reactions through conditioning procedures and the corollary conditions dealt with that have been identified.

RESPONDENT AND OPERANT TRACKS

The decision whether to pursue operant or respondent tracks to behavior change is very important. The complexity of this issue is best illustrated in an example of the treatment of a patient whose presenting complaint is anxiety but who, the behavioral analysis reveals, is also depressed. Since the treatment of anxiety may require the employment of deconditioning techniques based on respondent principles, while in the treatment of depression (where the assumption is made that the patient's condition is caused by a scarcity of positive reinforcements) procedures based on operant principles are employed, the question is where to begin first. Put another way, the question becomes one of whether (1) the individual is anxious in certain situations because of the absence of an effective repertoire of behavior for the attainment of an adequate amount of satisfaction and is left feeling helpless and fearful of coping with everyday tasks; or (2) learned anxiety reactions to a range of situations is so pervasive that the individual is inhibited from effectively moving out and obtaining the necessary gratifications in the first place. The clinician moves on both the respondent and operant tracks in a trial and error basis until it becomes clear where the best leverage for change lies. In the individual who is primarily depressed, operant procedures will ultimately prove the most effective. This will emerge empirically with the successful application of techniques where the individual's successes in effectively interacting with his environment will also be manifest in a reduction of anxiety symptoms. When anxiety reactions emerge as the primary disordered behavior, attempts at helping the patient move out to obtain reinforcements will prove to be unsuccessful, since the debilitating effect of inhibition will prove to be too much of a barrier. The clinician then will choose to concentrate on deconditioning maladaptive anxiety responses before he attempts to deal with his inadequate repertoire.

Another important consideration in designing the treatment strategy is the negative self-attitudes and irrational assumptions that the patient brings to the treatment situation. The therapist's efforts to institute changes will often not proceed well until these cognitive issues have been dealt with directly. The patient, for example, labels himself/herself a chronic failure of little worth with few of the abilities necessary to change the conditions of his/her life.

He/she has learned to denigrate any new effort he/she undertakes and anticipates failure. Procedures aimed at cognitive restructuring (Beck, 1976) through a direct focus on these irrational assumptions is necessary before the target behaviors themselves are broached through the introduction of various specific techniques.

THE TREATMENT PROCESS

The therapeutic hour provides the context for effecting changes in the patient's interaction with the environment, rather than the setting for effecting internal changes as in psychodynamic therapies. The work of therapy involves both replicative and instigative functions (Kanfer & Saslow, 1969). In the former the therapist employs techniques that replicate the patient's specific maladaptive reactions to interpersonal and physical situations in his life. The locus for change is the maladaptive feeling, thinking, and acting of the patient; the techniques employed are specific for each of these three modalities. The individual's anxiety, his/her irrational assumptions, or inappropriate actions become the targets for change. This replicative function of treatment is essentially a relearning one. In order for "corrective" experiences to occur, the therapist reproduces in the office the conditions that simulate those in the real situation. Systematic desensitization and assertive training are examples of these techniques. In systematic desensitization (Wolpe, 1973) a situation is designed in which the patient imagines real-world conditions that elicit disruptive emotional reactions, and experiences anxiety at controlled levels of intensity. Anxiety reactions are disassociated from these conditions (i.e., authority figures, high places, sexual situations, and others) through arranging for relaxed feelings to be associated instead with these stimuli in imagination. Generalization from the therapeutic situation to the real world then takes place. The patient, now free from anxiety, can enter these situations. In assertive training (Wolpe, 1973) the therapist rehearses with the patient, through role playing, appropriate responses in interpersonal situations. Appropriate adaptive behaviors are learned where previously the patient responded with inhibition, anxiety, and anger. In other words, the patient learns to be effective in interpersonal exchanges. He/she learns to express his/her feelings appropriately, to ask for what is needed, and to give what he/she wants to give. Satisfactions in interpersonal relations are in this manner increased and the subjective sense of "well-being" is enhanced.

Instigative functions involve teaching the patient ways of effecting changes directly in the interpersonal and physical environment outside the therapeutic situation. The therapist works with the patient's verbal description of the events in his/her life and identifies those conditions that are nonreinforcing or punishing. The goal is to make it possible for the patient to enter situations or to create new situations in his/her life that can provide adequate emotional and physical satisfactions. The socially inhibited patient, for example, is encouraged directly to seek out groups with which to associate. The therapist explores possible social contacts that are appropriate to the social and cultural background of the patient. In the employment area the therapist also explores appropriate changes, where indicated, that will enhance the effective functioning of the individual. Inhibitions that prevent realistic changes are dealt with as conditioned anxiety and appropriate deconditioning procedures are employed as part of the replicative functions carried out in the therapeutic situation. The acquisition of appropriate interpersonal skills, when necessary, also precedes changes in interpersonal situations and also constitutes a replicative function that is carried out in the office of the therapist.

This issue is further elaborated in the case of the male patient whose presenting problem is impotence, but who, the behavioral analysis reveals, is generally inhibited in the presence of women. In fact, he has very few social contacts with women at all. His interpersonal environment is limited to situations where he interacts with relatives and male friends. The therapeutic goals for this patient would involve deconditioning his anxiety reactions to the sexual situation itself. It would also be necessary for the patient to learn the appropriate interpersonal skills required in relating to women in order to expand his range of contacts. This would require going to social gatherings and other situations where the probability of meeting appropriate women would be high. Finding a woman with whom he could form a mutually reinforcing relationship, social as well as sexual, would complete the process of effective therapeutic change. The patient is now being maximally reinforced for appropriate, in this case, approach behaviors. The elimination of the symptom, impotence, constitutes the necessary precondition for change in his social (i.e., environmental) interactions.

In summary, replicative and instigative functions constitute two aspects of a single goal which is to bring about changes in the patient's interaction with the environment in a manner that results in an adequate amount of satisfaction in life.

CLINICAL NEGOTIATIONS OVER BEHAVIORAL TREATMENTS

The successful implementation of the clinical strategies described above is contingent on the degree to which therapist and client share certain common assumptions about the nature of the presenting problem, the goals of treatment, the methods to be employed in meeting those goals, and the conditions of the treatment process itself. Some of these were described in Chapter 1 where the "reculturization" process is discussed as an essential early step in the preparation for the implementation of the treatment strategy. Some additional issues will be described here that need to be negotiated for effective intervention to take place. Often those issues which cannot be resolved totally during the behavioral analysis stage of treatment will recur throughout the therapy, and so need to be addressed and resolved by the therapist and patient for the treatment to progress.

Often the patient's preparation for behavior therapy by the referring source will determine the patient's preconceptions of what to expect. For example, when the patient is referred with a specific symptom (such as a checking compulsion) the assumption is often made that the behavior therapist will eliminate it through the application of certain techniques requiring little or no effort from the individual. This expectation is analogous to that of the patient requiring surgery for the correction of a medical problem. When this expectation is frustrated by the therapist who expects the patient to adopt an active role in the treatment, a conflict will arise.

A variation of this issue is present in the patient who eschews psychodynamic therapy because he/she is not motivated to pursue the long introspective course this form of treatment requires. Often a patient is avoiding "looking at" the past or the current problem since to do so raises his/her anxiety level to uncomfortable proportions. The behavior therapist, again, is expected to make the problem go away with little or no cognitive or other effort on the patient's part. Often, in these cases, the patient has considered hypnosis as an alternative or has previously, unsuccessfully, tried this approach. Unless this discrepancy in mutual expectations is dealt with directly by the therapist and patient, communication will break down between them. This often occurs during the behavioral analysis stage of treatment when the therapist tries to take a history, or when the patient is asked to complete questionnaires or other data-gathering forms.

There is one additional variation of this issue that needs to be elaborated. It is the "when all else has failed" phenomenon. If a patient and his/her previous therapist considers that the patient is a "dropout" from psychodynamic therapy and that behavior therapy is the treatment of last resort, the perception of the "new" therapist will be affected accordingly. Expectations for change may be exaggerated and the frustration tolerance of the patient limited when treatment does not result in a rapid "cure." Therefore, this issue must be discussed in order for a more realistic posture to be assumed by the patient.

The issue of length of treatment is an issue that must be resolved early in the negotiations between therapist and patient. The therapist orients the patient to the task-oriented, time-limited nature of the therapeutic process. This orientation, however, needs to be tempered in those cases where it is interpreted to mean that his/her case will be concluded in a predetermined small number of sessions. The behavior therapy research literature certainly could lead one to this conclusion inappropriately. When the referring source has mediated this expectation to a potential behavior therapy patient, it must be explored by the therapist and dealt with early in the treatment process.

The issue of "control" is a critical one in behavior therapy. The patient whose previous conditioning history has aversely sensitized him/her to any effort to constrain his behavior will respond accordingly to the attempts of the therapist to implement a treatment strategy. This will become especially evident when the therapist attempts to make "contracts" with the patient to do certain things between appointments, such as practicing certain procedures. This effort constitutes a signal (a c.s.) for anxiety, and so is resisted overtly or covertly. Therefore, it becomes important that the therapist deal with this issue early in the negotiations. It is taken up directly and discussed in terms of the patient's choosing to delegate certain powers to the therapist over what he/she will or will not do. This power can be withdrawn by the patient at any time. The therapist, too, has the power not to continue treatment if the patient does not feel ready at that time to make changes by collaborating in the treatment. The therapist may also postpone any contracting until a therapeutic alliance is established and the patient is ready to "trust" the therapist. Once this alliance is solidified, the therapist is in a better position to negotiate contracts for specific behaviors beginning with least difficult and progressing to more radical changes. Much of what is labeled "resistance" in psychodynamic theory is dealt with in the context of the negotiated contract with the therapist. The therapist's message to the patient reads as follows: "Our relationship is based on the mutual expectation that each of us will contribute what we can to the behavioral change process." The therapist is expected to provide time, genuine caring, trust, technical expertise, structure, and continuous positive reinforcement for changes. The patient is expected to provide collaborative effort, trust, a willingness to take therapeutic risks, the willingness to raise doubts and anxious feelings with the therapist, a commitment to change, and a fee. Either of the two are justified in abrogating the therapeutic contract when these conditions are not met.

3
Behavioral Techniques

There is a continuing expansion of the technology employed in the implementation of behavior change strategies. Some techniques have been developed for employment in the modification of a broad range of behaviors, while others were designed for very specific disorders. In this chapter we will describe only those bedrock techniques that are in general use. The references that will be provided will guide the reader to those more esoteric techniques that he/she may have a desire to explore further.

In order to preserve the format used in the previous chapter on behavior therapy, techniques here are also categorized under cognitive, affective, and conative subheadings. However, since thinking, feeling, and acting are interactive processes, a technique designed to modify behavior in one of these categories will often be directed, in fact, to change in one of the other two. A technique employed to change the individual's irrational thinking, for example, may have as its ultimate purpose the amelioration of a disordered affective state. It is the differential use of these techniques in the context of the total treatment plan that must engage the clinical skill of the therapist.

TECHNIQUES DIRECTED TO THE MODIFICATION OF AFFECTIVE DYSFUNCTIONING

The development of techniques for the deconditioning of maladaptive anxiety reactions has occupied the attention of behavior therapists from the early days of the emergence of this modality of treatment. These techniques have been designed for the treatment of anxiety reactions to specific stimulus conditions termed "phobias" as well as to generalized anxiety and tension states. Relaxation training techniques are directed to the latter condition but are also employed in the treatment of specific phobias.

Relaxation Training Techniques

The purpose of these techniques is to teach the patient methods of deep physical relaxation. Since deep relaxation results in an autonomic state that is antithetical to that of anxiety and tension, it can be used to selectively control the latter condition in some patients.

Edmund Jacobson first employed "progressive relaxation" as the treatment of choice for a broad range of neurotic disorders. The original work in which this method was described appeared in the 1938 book *Progressive Relaxation*. The technique was revived by Wolpe who incorporated it as the initial step in the "systematic desensitization" procedure which he developed for the treatment of specific phobic reactions and which will be described below. A shortened version of Jacobson's relaxation method is described by Wolpe (1973). The subject is instructed, step by step, to tense and then relax the various muscle groupings in his body in a sequential manner. In about six therapeutic sessions, with practice periods between sessions at home, the subject can be trained to achieve deep levels of relaxation.

Once the training is completed and practiced on a regular basis each day the individual learns the "habit" of relaxation so that the ability is acquired to counteract anxiety arousal in specific situations with a relaxation response. One can "turn on" the relaxation response in the anxiety situation itself by self-statements, such as "I am relaxed," that have become associated with the relaxation of muscle groupings during the training exercises. Another technique used to "turn on" relaxation involves the individual's relaxing specific muscles differentially (leg or arm). A generalization effect results so that his/her entire body becomes relaxed in a short period of time. The availability of this technique to a patient provides him/her with a method for relaxing in a variety of situations. It can be employed to reduce the accumulated tensions of the day, as a method for preparing oneself for entering stressful situations, and in general as a prophylactic measure to be used for preventing the inordinate arousal of anxiety in conditions previously associated with this response. The mechanics of Jacobson's progressive relaxation training are described also by Goldfried and Davison (1976). There are several taped versions of relaxation training on the market in cassette form (Evans, ed., 1975–1976).

A second major relaxation method is described in Benson's book, *The Relaxation Response* (1975). This method, based on the transcendental meditation method of intoning a word subvocally, is described by Benson, an internist, who conducted an extensive research program on its use with cardiac patients at the Beth Israel Hospital in Boston. In contrast to the Jacobsonian method, it can be learned in a few minutes and it results in the same deep levels of relaxation with the accompanying lowering of heart rate, blood pressure, and skin resistance associated with the *progressive relaxation* method

(Greenwood & Benson, 1977, pp. 337–343). It can, furthermore, be effective with some patients who do not respond to progressive relaxation. I have found that some patients with tendencies to obsess and ruminate a great deal cannot be relaxed with the Jacobsonian method but do respond to Benson's technique. On the other hand, other patients become fearful of "losing control" when asked to close their eyes and repeat the word "one." I switch these patients to the progressive relaxation method.

The mechanics of this technique are described by Benson:

1. Sit quietly in a comfortable position.
2. Close your eyes.
3. Deeply relax all your muscles, beginning at your feet and progressing up to your face. Keep them relaxed.
4. Breathe through your nose. Become aware of your breathing. As you breathe out, say the word, "ONE," silently to yourself. For example, breathe IN . . . OUT, "ONE"; IN . . . OUT, "ONE"; and so forth. Breathe easily and naturally.
5. Continue for 10 to 20 minutes. You may open your eyes to check the time, but do not use an alarm. When you finish, sit quietly for several minutes, at first with your eyes closed and later with your eyes opened. Do not stand up for a few minutes.
6. Do not worry about whether you are successful in achieving a deep level of relaxation. Maintain a passive attitude and permit relaxation to occur at its own pace. When distracting thoughts occur, try to ignore them by not dwelling upon them and return to repeating "ONE." With practice, the response should come with little effort. Practice the technique once or twice daily, but not within two hours after any meal, since the digestive processes seem to interfere with the elicitation of the Relaxation Response [Benson, 1975].

Benson's research on this method of relaxation has shown that over time it serves to raise an individual's threshold for stress. It serves to "immunize" the individual from inordinate anxiety reactions to previously conditioned stimuli. I have found this method to be an important adjunct in implementing behavior change programs in a variety of different neurotic disorders. The patient is provided with a technique to facilitate the change process by reducing the stress, i.e., anxiety and tension, involved in the process. Patients who have practiced Benson's relaxation response for a period of time are able to rapidly relax themselves by repeating the word "one" to themselves just before they are about to enter an anxiety producing situation, or when they suddenly feel anxiety coming on without any apparent external environmental cue that it is about to happen. I have also used it as the preparatory step in the employment of systematic desensitization technique in the place of Jacobson's progressive relaxation response.

Corbett and Corbett's (1976) *relaxation therapy* method constitutes a significant advance in relaxation training procedures. This technique incorporates and integrates three approaches to relaxation. These are abbreviated progressive relaxation, relaxation via sensory awareness, and the employment of covert reinforcing processes. In a 12-step training program the subject is instructed in the utilization of these three modalities—physical relaxation, autogenic feedback, and the imagining of relaxing scenes. This program has been carefully researched and provides the subject with detailed instructions for implementing it. The instruction booklet is supplemented by an audio cassette which the subject plays as he traverses the steps of the relaxation training. A film that provides the visual imagery accompanying the auditory instructions of the audio portion is available for group and individual use.

This method has proven effective with patients who are unable to "get into" either Jacobson's progressive relaxation or Benson's relaxation response. It provides considerably more "structure" and the multimodal feature of the program enhances the probability that complete relaxation can be achieved.

Systematic Desensitization

Systematic desensitization is the classical deconditioning technique designed by Wolpe (1973) for the treatment of anxiety reactions or "phobias" to specific situations. It is also employed in the treatment of interpersonal anxiety (fear of authority figures, fear of sexual situations) and for anxiety conditions where the cues are "endogenous" (fear aroused by bodily cues, such as heartbeat). In fact, it has also been employed in the treatment of anxiety-evoking "thoughts" such as "I am going crazy." The animal research on which this technique is based and the principle of reciprocal inhibition, which is employed to explain its counterconditioning effects, was described earlier. A detailed description of both the theoretical underpinnings of this technique and the mechanics of its application are well described by Wolpe (1973).

The employment of this technique involves four major steps:

1. Training in deep muscle relaxation.
2. The construction of anxiety hierarchies.
3. Imaginal training.
4. Counterposing relaxation and anxiety-evoking stimuli.

The first step, Jacobson's progressive relaxation method, has been described above. The second step involves identifying those anxiety-arousing situations that are activating the anxiety reactions. The patient is first asked to list the concrete situations where he/she has been anxious in the past (elevators, talking to the boss, before taking a trip, studying for an exam). These concrete situations are then reorganized according to themes. For example, fear of enclosed places and fear of elevators may both be categorized under the same theme "claustrophobia." The next step involves discriminating the exact stimuli in those situations that activate the anxiety reactions. A person may report he/she is afraid of criticism, but on closer scrutiny it becomes evident that this fear is activated specifically in the work situation and in the context of relating to male authority figures. A fear of birds may involve a variety of parameters such as the kind of bird, distance from the patient, direction of flight, and whether the patient is alone or not. Once these variables have been identified, the concrete situations encompassed by each theme are ordered on a hierarchy of intensity of the anxiety reaction they elicit. The therapist asks the patient to rate on a scale of 0 to 100 (with 100 representing blind panic) how much anxiety each of the situations arouses. The subjective units of disturbance (s.u.d.s) assigned by the patient to each of the situations determines their relative position on that particular thematic hierarchy, which is usually comprised of about eight or ten situations or scenes.

The third step involves teaching the patient to turn on in his imagination a neutral anxiety-free scene, and then to focus on those scenes in which the relevant anxiety-evoking stimuli are focused on. The preliminary training involves teaching the patient to construct a scene in his/her imagination piecemeal by utilizing all relevant sensory modalities (visual cues, sounds, odors, proprioceptive cues, and others) so that the experience achieved is of really being in the situation. When this is done properly the patient usually also experiences the accompanying feeling, i.e., anxiety. Patients often improve remarkably in their capacity to imagine scenes with repeated practice.

The major therapeutic work is done in this fourth and final step. The patient is first relaxed to the point where he reports experiencing less than 10 degrees (or s.u.d.s) of anxiety. The patient is then instructed to turn on the scene lowest in the hierarchy of a particular theme. When the patient experiences anxiety a signal (raised forefinger) is given to the therapist who times the exposure to the anxiety scene. Length of exposure varies up to about 15 seconds. Shorter exposure times in this general range are used to keep the anxiety arousal level to around 30 or 40 s.u.d.s. Longer exposures of up to 15 seconds are employed when the anxiety arousal potential has been determined to be in the desired 30-40 s.u.d.s range.

The patient is next instructed to turn off the scene and relax deeply. When the patient indicates that a relaxed state has again been achieved, the therapist turns on the same scene again. After repeated trials on the same scene the counterconditioning effects should, if it is working, manifest themselves in progressively lowered reported anxiety arousal levels. (The patient is asked periodically how much anxiety a just experienced scene evoked.) When the patient reports that the scene now elicits little (under 10 s.u.d.s) or no anxiety the therapist moves one scene up on the hierarchy, and so forth until all the items are covered.

A desensitization session lasts usually for about 20-30 minutes; longer than that will tax the concentration of most patients. More than one scene from two or more hierarchies can be worked on alternatively in the same desensitization hierarchy to counteract boredom.

Transference of desensitization to the real situation occurs. There is sometimes a time lag between desensitization in imagination and its transference to the real situation.

The patient is contracted to go into the real phobic situation after his/her anxiety has been reduced so sufficiently in imagination that the individual feels ready to attempt it. In this variation of the classical implementation of the procedure, the patient may not in fact have reached a 0–10 s.u.d.'s level of anxiety arousal, so that the *in vivo* exposure or partial "flooding" is expected to account for the final neutralization or "extinction" of the anxiety response.

Flooding

This technique involves exposing the patient to phobic situations, either in imagination (*in vitro*) or in the real situation (*in vivo*), so that high levels of anxiety arousal are reached. "Extinction" of the anxiety response is theorized to occur during long exposure times to the anxiety-evoking stimulus conditions (c.s.), when a diminution of subjectively felt fear is observed to occur.

The rationale for this treatment has been elaborated by Stamphl (1967, pp. 496–503), who employs both learning theory and psychoanalytic theory, in conceptualizing the operations employed in "implosion," as he has labeled his procedure. Implosion, which is done exclusively in imagination, involves guiding the patient from exposure to the immediate anxiety-provoking stimulus conditions (high places) to the experience of anxiety associated with progressively lower levels of psychosexual development (castration anxiety, oral deprivation, and total abandonment). A small number of long "implosion sessions" is reported by him to result in pervasive and long-standing behavioral changes.

Flooding is employed in the treatment of phobias and obsessive-compulsive reactions by a group of researchers at the Mauseley Hospital in London (Marks, 1969). Their procedures exclusively employ *in vivo,* or real life, situations. In the treatment of phobic reactions, the patients are brought into direct contact with the situations that caused them to feel anxious and that they have consequently avoided for long periods of time, years in many cases. Agoraphobic patients are taken as a group on a bus into London and instructed to venture into the streets. Initial panic is followed by a progressive decrease in the subjectively felt anxiety during a surprisingly small number of "treatment" sessions. A hospital mental health worker, not necessarily a doctor, provides encouragement and reassurance as patients make repeated forays on successive days into streets and squares where before they could not venture.

The treatment of contamination phobias or obsessive-compulsive syndromes follows the same exposure principles (Marks, Hodgson, & Rachman, 1975, pp. 349-364; Rachman, Hodgson, & Marks, 1971, pp. 237-247; 1972, pp. 181-189; Roper, Rachman, & Hodgson, 1973, pp. 271-272). The patient, on an inpatient basis, is exposed to the conditions that evoke intense anxiety (such as dirt, touching others, and "contaminated" clothes). The patient is encouraged to come in contact with the contaminated objects and then is prevented from engaging in the decontamination rituals previously employed for anxiety relief such as hand washing, bathing, checking, and others. Repeated exposure with prevention of anxiety relief responses results in the elimination of pervasive and long term compulsions in a small number of treatment sessions.

TECHNIQUES DIRECTED TO THE MODIFICATION OF COGNITIVE PROCESSES

Techniques employed for the direct modification of cognitive processes have emerged more recently in behavior therapy (Mahoney, 1974, 1979; Meichenbaum, 1977). Cognitive events, many of which are nonverbalized beliefs, were not originally considered to fall within the realm of behavior therapy, whose distinctive focus was external observable behavioral events. It has more recently been argued, however, that the human organism's responses to environmental events are mediated through cognitive processes. These cognitive processes "structure" or give "meaning" to those events, and so themselves constitute "behavior" that lends itself to modification.

The term "cognitive behavior therapy" is used to separate this approach from more classical "respondent" and "operant" tracks described above.

Cognitive behavioral techniques are centered on changing the maladaptive thinking patterns individuals have acquired in response to external events. It is not the events themselves, it is argued, that cause disordered affective responses such as anxiety, rage, and depression; but the self-statements that an individual makes before, during, and after experiencing those events. Meichenbaum describes a retraining program in which he teaches individuals (1) to substitute alternative positive, i.e., "rational," self-statements when approaching a potentially anxiety generating situation; (2) to actively produce these alternative cognitions during the experiencing of the anxiety; and (3) to reinforce themselves with self-rewarding statements when they succeed in managing the situation in this manner. He also teaches his subjects to relax themselves physically before and after entering an anxiety-evoking situation in order to reduce the endogenous, i.e., autonomic, cues associated with anx-

iety arousal. The same cognitive restructuring techniques have been employed successfully in the management of anger and pain. Meichenbaum and
his associates have applied these techniques to a broad range of individuals
with problems in these areas, including institutionalized psychotic patients.

The current cognitive behavior therapy approach was pioneered by Albert
Ellis (1962, 1980). His "rational-emotive" therapy is focused on helping the
individual become aware of irrational assumptions or beliefs that underscore inappropriate emotional reactions to specific events. Ellis lists specific
irrational assumptions that are characteristic of individuals in our society.
The following are two examples of these assumptions: (1) The idea that it is a
dire necessity for an adult human being to be loved or approved by virtually
every significant other person in his community; (2) The idea that one should
be thoroughly competent, adequate, and achieving in all possible respects if
one is to consider oneself worthwhile. The therapist who applies this rational-
emotive approach is taught specific interviewing skills through which he/she
can help the patient become aware of irrational beliefs that are patterning his
emotional reactions to life events. The patient is thereby "freed" to assess
new situations rationally and, therefore, without activating disruptive affective responses.

The work of Beck (1976) in the treatment of depression is based on cogni-
tive-restructuring approaches and has drawn wide attention because of the
impressive therapeutic results that he has been able to achieve.

The work of Cautela (1967, pp. 459–468; 1969; 1970, pp. 33–50) and Cautela and Bennett (1981) on covert conditioning techniques in the treatment of
a broad range of neurotic disorders also belongs under the heading of cognitive approaches. His procedures are based on the assumption that stimuli presented in the imagination through instructions have similar functional relationships to overt and covert behaviors as do stimuli presented externally. He
has labeled his procedures covert sensitization, covert positive reinforcement, covert negative reinforcement, and covert extinction.

In covert sensitization the individual is instructed to imagine that he is receiving noxious stimulation whenever he is able to perform an undesirable
behavior. In the treatment of alcoholism, for example, the patient is instructed first in imaginal techniques so he feels the glass, smells and tastes the
liquor of his choice. When he indicates (with his eyes closed and imagining
the relevant event actually occurring) that he has swallowed the liquid, he is
instructed to imagine that he is feeling sick and is guided through the entire sequence of vomiting response with all the accompanying physical and olfac-
tory cues. The aversive consequence (vomiting) is made to follow the drinking response in the same way that an aversive chemical agent (antabuse) or a
physical agent (faradic shock) is employed in aversive treatments.The frequency of the drinking response is thereby decreased. It has been demonstrated that generalization to the real situation then occurs as in systematic desensitization.

In covert positive reinforcement the frequency of a desirable behavior is increased in the same manner by arranging for a positive reinforcing consequence to occur when it is performed in imagination. The shy male is instructed to imagine calling a girl he wants to date. This "calling a girl" behavior is broken down into its component parts (walking to the phone, dialing the appropriate number, hearing himself make opening remarks, and others). After the patient has imagined himself in each of these situations in sequence and experienced the associated feelings, he is instructed to turn off the particular scene and immediately turn on an alternative positive pleasure-inducing one. This reinforcing scene is practiced beforehand so that it can be readily imaged with the associated positive affect. A typical reinforcing scene that is often used is lying on the beach relaxing with warm sun pouring on one's body and the sound of the ocean in the background. Since each of the steps in the behavioral sequence "calling up a girl for a date" is now associated with the positive affect or reinforcement, it becomes possible to execute it in the real situation since the previously inhibiting anxiety has become dissociated from those responses.

Covert negative reinforcement and covert extinction employ paralleled procedures in which the relevant learning principles are brought to bear in the modification of the target behaviors.

Covert behavioral techniques have also been employed by Suinn (1975) in innovative programs to modify maladaptive anxiety reactions in patients and recently in the modification control of disruptive feelings in athletes performing in highly competitive events such as alpine skiing (Suinn, 1972).

TECHNIQUES DIRECTED TO THE MODIFICATION OF DISORDERED CONATIVE RESPONSES

The conative category encompasses here a broad range of behaviors. It includes discrete motor responses such as nervous tics (Hersen & Eisler, 1973), trichotillomania (Rosenbaum & Ayllon, 1981), nail biting (Davidson, Denny, & Elliot, 1980), enuresis (Doleys, 1977); a second more complex class of behaviors such as addictions, i.e., smoking (Poole, Sauson-Fishen, & German, 1981), drinking or drug abuse (Miller & Fox, 1981), sexual deviations (Adams, Tollison, & Carson, 1981); and finally a third, still more complex, class of behaviors labeled "inhibitory" where the individual is unable to emit the appropriate responses in specific situations. This latter group includes lack of assertion in interpersonal relationships, impotence and frigidity in the sexual situation, the inability to produce in creative efforts such as writing and painting when productive output is "blocked off." This latter category includes only those disorders in which the individual has acquired the appropriate repertoire of behavior in the past but is unable to perform in the present. On the other hand, individuals who may be deficient in the skills necessary for adequate performance present a different kind of conative problem. Often, however, there is a mixture of inhibition and behavioral deficit in the presenting problem behaviors so that the therapist needs to sort out the differences and apply appropriate techniques for change.

The techniques employed in the modification of concrete, circumscribed behaviors are designed to both decrease the rate at which the undesirable behavior occurs and to increase the rate of occurrence of a competing, adaptive, substitute response. The aversion methods to decrease the rate of undesirable behaviors have been used widely and effectively in the treatment of a broad range of behaviors including those more complex addictive behaviors noted above. (A comprehensive review of aversion methods in behavior therapy is provided by Sandler [1975].) The therapy involves arranging conditions so that the undesirable behavior is followed by a noxious "punishing" outcome. A variety of aversive consequences have been employed, the most common being electrical (faradic shock) and chemical (nausea-producing drugs). The early use of antabuse in the treatment of alcoholism is an example of the latter. Electric shock has been employed in the treatment of sexual deviations, alcoholism, and other "compulsive"-like behaviors.

The use of some aversion methods has drawn criticism because of their potential for infringement of individual rights so that substitute techniques have been advocated by behavior therapists. Azrin and Nunn (1973, pp. 619–628) advocate a program that maximizes the use of the principle of "overcorrection" in the treatment of enuresis and other nonadaptive behaviors in retarded and hospitalized mentally ill populations. Substitute adaptive behaviors become the focus of the retraining program in which the individual learns to perform the desired behaviors (urinating in the bathroom) at a high rate. The need for punishment is thereby eliminated.

Cautela's covert sensitization technique, described above, also eliminates the need for the employment of chemical and electrical aversion methods. He describes its use in the treatment of alcoholism and cigarette smoking and other undesirable behaviors.

Obsessive-compulsive behaviors (Sturgis & Meyer, 1981), such as hand washing and checking, are clearly conative disorders. Their treatment was discussed above in the section on techniques employed in the treatment of affective disorders. The patient is prevented from engaging in rituals that result in anxiety relief and are thereby reinforcing (negative reinforcement). The resulting subjectively experienced anxiety is allowed to increase in intensity. In the absence of negative reinforcement (anxiety relief through performance of the rituals), the anxiety response decreases or is extinguished and the patient's compulsion is eliminated. The prevention of anxiety-relieving rituals acts as a kind of aversive consequence to the initial compulsive drive and thereby reduces further the rate of occurrence of the compulsive act. How much of the elimination of the compulsive behavior is attributable to extinction of the anxiety response and how much to aversive deconditioning of the compulsive act itself is unclear (Rachman, Hodgson, & Marks, 1971, pp. 237–247).

Once compulsive behaviors of the discrete variety described above or those involving a more complex configuration of behaviors such as drug addiction are reduced in rate of occurrence, alternative competing reinforcing behaviors must be increased in the life of the patient. The therapist, in the behavioral analysis, has determined what available potentially reinforcing behaviors the patient has in his/her behavioral repertoire. Direct encouragement is used to instigate the patient to engage in these reinforcing behaviors. The patient may be "contracted" to engage in these substitute behaviors at a prescribed time and with a prescribed frequency. Contracting is a technique in which the patient agrees to perform certain behaviors between therapeutic sessions. The patient grants to the therapist the "power" to expect him to meet the terms of the contract and adheres to previously agreed on penalties if he fails to do so.

The treatment of stuttering has been researched in depth by Brady (1971, p. 2) who has devised a metronome technique as part of a total therapeutic program. He describes his method in several publications.

That broad class of disorders resulting from the inhibition of adaptive responses in interpersonal situations has engaged the attention of behavior therapists from the early days of this movement's emergence. The early work of Salter (1949) on what has since come to be known as "assertion training" pioneered the way of interacting effectively with others in interpersonal situations. Lazarus (1971), Fersterheim and Baer (1975), and others have since elaborated the original principles of Salter in teaching individuals to effectively assert their legitimate needs and to assure that these needs are met in interactions with significant others in their interpersonal environment. The major principle undergirding this approach is that individuals have been conditioned in the past to feeling anxious when they attempt to move in the direction of meeting their basic psychological needs. They characteristically defer to others, at first to parents and siblings and then to friends and lovers and spouses and children, so that their personal gratifications are systematically structured out of their lives. The resulting paucity of reinforcement results in the broad variety of neurotic disorders from psychosomatic problems to sexual inadequacy. Assertion training is designed to teach the individual to progressively desensitize himself/herself to inhibitory anxiety through the act of asserting himself/herself in interpersonal situations in a graduated fashion paralleling the systematic desensitization paradigm described above. In assertion training, the neutralization of anxiety occurs through actually behaving affirmatively in the real situation. Careful attention is paid to differentiating assertion from aggressive responses since the latter will invite counter-aggression and therefore have an aversive consequence, while the former will result in the acquisition of positive reinforcement (Twentyman & Zimering, 1979).

The therapist teaches the patient in the office through "modeling" the appropriate assertive behavior and through "role playing," where the opportunity is provided for actually practicing behaving in an assertive manner. The therapist feeds back corrective reactions to the patient's assertive performance, commenting on voice intonations, facial appearance, and body posture, until the patient has perfected an appropriate repertoire which can be employed effectively outside the office.

Modeling as a behavior modification technique has been researched extensively by Bandura (1969) who has demonstrated its effectiveness in a variety of clinical settings. A summary review of the basic work on "modeling" by Marlatt and Perry (1975) can be found in Kanfer and Goldstein (1975). A detailed description of the use of role playing in assertion training can be found in a chapter entitled, "Simulation and Role Playing Methods," by John V. Flowers (1975), also in Kanfer and Goldstein. The patient is also reinforced by the therapist to take assertive postures in modifying his lifestyle by identifying goals and implementing a systematic program of concentrated effort for their attainment.

This aspect of therapy has been labeled "problem-solving" by Goldfried and Davison (1976). They have elaborated a systematic approach to decision making and the other important steps to actively engaging the "real" problems that confront people. The "problem-solving" approach is consistent, of course, with the major thrust of the behavior therapeutic effort to facilitate the individual's effective interaction with the environment. This effort involves the acquisiton of problem solving skills necessary for successful adaptation to a complex social environment.

The treatment of sexual dysfunction through behavioral methods has been an early focus of the conditioning therapies. Impotence and frigidity are conceptualized as conditions in which the sexual situation has become associated with the arousal of anxiety that inhibits sexual response. Sexual arousal is primarily a parasympathetic function, while anxiety is a sympathetic function.

Therapeutic intervention is designed to reverse the original learning or conditioning in which these connections were formed. The sexual response itself is employed as the anxiety inhibitor. The patient is instructed to preplan sexual encounters with the partner in a manner designed to make sexual stimulation occur at a higher intensity than the corollary anxiety that is aroused in the situation. This is accomplished by instructing the partner to stimulate the patient in a graded, stepwise fashion that parallels the procedure described above in systematic desensitization. The sexual stimulation in this procedure substitutes for the relaxation response in systematic desensitization. Intercourse is attempted only after the intermediary steps, such as foreplay, mounting the partner, and insertion, have been systematically and successfully performed (Masters & Johnson, 1970).

The utilization of behavioral techniques in the treatment of a broad range of health related disorders has become the focus of "behavioral medicine" in recent years. This approach has stimulated a wide range of relevant clinical research that has resulted in a corollary broad range of methods in the treatment of various medical problems such as vascular disorders (Kallman & Gilmore, 1981), paroxysmal disorders of the central nervous system (Mostofsky, 1981), and migraine headaches (Blanchard et al., 1980). A comprehensive review of this area is provided by Melamed and Siegel (1980).

4
Clinical Issues

In this chapter some of the basic clinical issues confronted in intensive therapy will be reviewed from a behavioral perspective. The intention here is to conceptualize these issues in terms of a behavioral theoretical frame of reference and to describe intervention strategies that are consistent with this understanding. It will become evident that the effort here is different from that of Dollard and Miller (1950) who translated psychoanalytic understandings of these issues into learning theory terms. Freud first identified processes such as transference, resistance, and defense, and interpreted them in terms of the theoretical framework he developed. His pioneering discoveries, however, do not make the issues themselves "Freudian" anymore than the concept of "reinforcement" is Thorndikian or Skinnerian. The major difference is that Freud, and Dollard and Miller focused their conceptualizations entirely on intraindividual processes. The cognitions and emotions of the patient as he/she produced them in the course of the therapeutic hour became the subject matter of their analytic and therapeutic activity. This is not the case in behavior therapy. These productions of the patient constitute one facet of an interaction process, with environmental events constituting the other part. Helping a person change his/her "head" (modes of thinking and feeling without attending to those environmental conditions that they are thinking and feeling a reaction to) is to engage in a minimally effective therapeutic process.

Individuals indeed acquire consistent modes of thinking, feeling, and acting that psychodynamicists have labeled with nosological categories such as obsessive-compulsive or hysterical. The functional relationship of these cognitive, effective and conative habits to the social and physical conditions in which they live is not included in their theoretical formulations, however. A person with compulsive "traits," for example, relates to a kind of job that will support his "habit," marries a spouse who will endure it, and chooses a

36

lifestyle that will not interfere with it. These are the "environmental" counterparts to compulsive thinking that need to be addressed therapeutically if permanent change is to be effected. These are "reinforcing conditions" that maintain the patient's habit and need to be changed if this compulsiveness is to be neutralized. Changing his "head" may be a necessary, but not sufficient, condition for change.

The behavioral reconceptualization of some classical clinical issues and the strategies developed for their management is based on certain theoretical assumptions which need to be elaborated first. The following brief development of this theoretical position was not intended to be either comprehensive in its scope nor definitive in its ordering of all the relevant clinical parameters. Furthermore, it is a "clinical formulation" based on one behavioral clinician's understanding of what goes on in the clinical process. It was arrived at as were many of the other formulations provided here—through intensive exposure to the complex clinical issues presented by patients struggling with crippling inhibition and anxiety.

A central feature of this theoretical formulation are the concepts of entrapment and abandonment. They constitute bipolar positions on an anxiety parameter that is understood to reflect the unconditional phylogenetically determined fear of death. This fear has the obvious adaptive function of assuring the physical survival of the organism as in other species. In humans, physical survival is indeed contingent on the nurturing function of parents or parent surrogates. The sense of psychological security, i.e., the sense of being safe, is acquired through the physical presence of parent surrogates who minister to the physical and biological needs of the maturing individual. Loving and caring for the child (i.e., attention, interest, physical touching, and caressing) becomes in time an individual source of psychological nurturing equally necessary for both physical and emotional survival. The threat of loss of love activates primitive fears of separation and death. The fears of patients often include fantasies of being left destitute and dying (Bowlby, 1973; Mahler, Pine, & Bergman, 1975).

It is in the subjectively experienced feeling of "helplessness" that fears of entrapment and abandonment become manifest. (Seligman [1975] has elaborated the concept of "learned" helplessness and has given empirical support to the conditions of its acquisition in an extensive program of animal research.) Individuals whose early, formative experiences in the home involved learning to interact with their environment in a manner that effectively assured reinforcing consequences are thereby immunized from the primitive fears of entrapment and abandonment. These interactions with the environment include both the skillful performance of concrete tasks of a physical and intellectual kind, as well as the effective contracting of satisfying interpersonal relationships. They have learned they can always do something to cope with difficult and threatening situations. It takes extreme crises to activate in them these primitive fears. They can do most of what they want to and have learned to invest in others and enjoy the satisfaction of being cared for.

In others, whose early experiences were devoid of opportunities to learn effective skills required for daily living including both those necessary for the performance of concrete tasks and those that constitute investment in interpersonal relationships, have a very low threshold for anxiety. They are easily threatened by cues of being trapped in a job they worry they cannot perform well, or in a relationship they fear will engulf them and deprive them of the psychological space to be "free"—that is, to exist. They also worry about being abandoned by others. Social disapproval becomes a life-threatening condition. They can never really "trust" others who potentially can turn on them or abandon them. The conditions where dread could be activated in the person conditioned to feel helpless are myriad in a complex achievement oriented society where individualism is a highly valued personal trait. The assertiveness of others is processed as aggression, and the individual's own anger in response to frustrating situations is processed as threatening since it can result in retaliatory acts from those about whom it is felt.

Individuals manage to cope with this experienced state of affairs by avoiding those situations where they experience anxiety. They carve out, so to speak, a psychological space where they feel safe. This often reflects a truncated lifestyle devoid of satisfactions that result from accepting job challenges, risking emotional relationships, and from realizing the potential with which they were endowed.

The above formulation constitutes the rationale on which intervention strategies are based. The objective of the therapist becomes that of stimulating the patient to move into situations that activate fears of entrapment and abandonment. The confrontation of these situations becomes the basis of the therapeutic process—the condition for therapeutic change. This process involves arranging for anxiety to be experienced under controlled conditions and in a graded stepwise fashion. This exposure to anxiety-evoking events serves to "extinguish," or erode, the individual's sensitivity, or low threshold to anxiety reactions in these situations. This "extinction" principle is the same as that undergirding the rationale behind specific techniques (for example, "systematic desensitization" and "implosion") employed in the elimination of discrete symptoms, such as phobias and compulsions. The utilization of this "extinction" principle is not limited, however, to specific techniques employed in the elimination of specific symptoms. It is employed in the broader scope of facilitating movement toward and confrontation with a wide range of anxiety-evoking conditions in the life of the patient. Specific symptoms interfere with this movement and so have to be dealt with separately. Basic change occurs in the direct, satisfying experience of previously avoided situations outside the therapy office that relate to love and work. Inhibitory anxiety becomes eliminated when the individual is able to repeatedly enter these situations where anxiety is progessively diminished.

Exposure to anxiety-evoking conditions is the necessary, but not sufficient, contingency on which change is based. The patient must possess the necessary behavioral repertoire for succeeding in these previously avoided situations. This obvious fact is often overlooked by therapists planning a treatment strategy. Fear of committing oneself to a heterosexual situation may be partly based in some individuals on a total ignorance of the mechanical skills one needs to have acquired for effective and satisfying lovemaking. Avoidance of specific situations may be based less on fear of authority and more on realistic facts; for example, the individual does not possess the necessary interpersonal, as well as the concrete work skills, to perform effectively in that work. Therefore, the acquisition of requisite skills in these cases must constitute the first order of therapeutic business before "exposure" to the relevant situation is attempted.

TRANSFERENCE

It has been elaborated by Freud and made the cornerstone of his theory that patients transfer to the therapist thoughts and feelings and behavior originally learned in interactions with their parents. Indeed, the major work of psychoanalytic therapy involves the patient's successfully "working through"; that is, making progressively finer cognitive discriminations between those associations acquired early in childhood in relation to parental figures and the "reality" that characterizes the therapist as a person. This newly acquired "insight" is, then, hopefully utilized by the patient in his/her interactions with people outside the therapy office for more reality oriented and conflict free interpersonal relationships. While the formulation may apply more to classical psychoanalysis and less to psychoanalytically oriented therapy where the focus is on "ego functioning" (that is, how the patient is managing what is really going on in his/her life), the interpretation of the phenomenon is the same.

In Behavior Therapy, the issue is not one of simply translating the term "transference" to "generalization" which is the learning theory equivalent. There is no question that the patient will generalize early conditioned modes of thinking, feeling, and acting to the therapist. That is to say, there is no question that this will occur if certain corollary conditions are also met. The therapist, first of all, must reinforce this process by remaining relatively passive in the therapeutic interaction. Secondly, the patient must be "reculturized" to focusing on the relationship to the therapist as the locus where therapeutic change occurs. This, indeed, is what a significant portion of therapeutic interactions are devoted to in psychoanalytically oriented therapies.

Since these two requisite conditions are not met in behavior therapy, the outcome (that is, the "resolution of the transference neurosis") takes a very different course. The therapist, first of all, is active, not passive. He/she assumes the role of an expert consultant allied with the patient to effect more adaptive interactions with his/her social and physical environment. The locus of treatment, therefore, also mitigates against the reinforcement of the transference-generalization phenomenon. Energies of both therapist and patient are centered on learning new ways to deal with conflictive situations in the interpersonal environment. When this process succeeds and the individual is more effective in cooperative work, in more gratifying interpersonal relationships, in better sexual relationships, and others, the early conditioned distorted cognitive and emotional reactions dissipate. The appropriate, reality oriented, discriminations follow behavioral change rather than precede it. This is the crux of the difference between the two approaches. It is also a difference that is theoretically consistent within the two psychotherapeutic systems. It makes sense that this outcome would occur from a learning theory, here a principally "operant" or "Skinnerian" perspective and equally impossible from a psychoanalytic (i.e., Freudian) frame of reference.

The achievement of therapeutic goals in behavior therapy rarely proceeds in the straightforward manner suggested above. The patient may, indeed, enter the therapeutic situation in the first instance with a cognitive set that will retard the progress in treatment unless it is dealt with directly. The patient, for example, may expect the behavior therapist to assume a rigidly authoritarian posture that would be consistent with his/her past experience with parental figures. For example, the patient's learned modes of dealing with authority figures may be limited to hostile emotional responses, passive compliance, or both; and may be employed simultaneously (passive-aggressive), or alternately hostile in some situations and anxiously compliant (passive dependent) in others. Therefore the therapist's efforts to do a behavioral analysis and design a treatment strategy are met with hostile, noncooperative reactions in the patient or passivity of such a pervasive nature that effective change is precluded from occurring. The patient announces that he/she is not going to be controlled by an authoritarian, i.e., behavior therapist who is dictating what he/she will do. The patient is also prepared to battle with the therapist when unrealistic expectations are not met. The patient expects to be "cured" without any effort on his/her part. That, after all, is why behavior therapy was chosen over other forms of treatment—that is to say, an immediate "magical change" is expected to occur of the kind patients experienced as children when they were hurt or when they needed something. The parent was always there to provide.

These transference phenomena are dealt with in the context of the therapeutic alliance. The therapist may choose to postpone undertaking any of the operations included in the therapeutic program until the patient, in the course of several sessions, has the opportunity to experience the therapist as a "real" person. During this relationship-building phase, the therapist makes direct cognitive inputs, interpretations if you prefer, through which he/she challenges the irrational assumptions of the patient described above. Thus there is an affective experiential component and a cognitive factor involved in dealing with the transference phenomenon. There is a conative factor as well; the therapist behaves in an open, forthright, and honest manner in his interactions with the patient. Long silences are never endured by the patient. The therapist is always actively working with him/her to examine irrational assumptions and to convey positive feelings of "investment" in the interests of the patient. The objective is to "free" the patient in a gradual manner, cognitively and affectively and conatively so that he/she is prepared to proceed with the major work of treatment that will lead to the desired changes.

RESISTANCE

The successful management of the transference phenomenon and the opening of the way to implementing the treatment program does not, of course, resolve once and for all the "resistance" to change that inevitably will recur as the therapy progresses. The therapist can count on it especially when it is progressing well and the patient is confronting those conditions in his/her environment in which anxiety and other maladaptive and painful emotional reactions are aroused. The patient will mobilize all those previously learned responses, including those discussed above as transference phenomenon, to avoid those conditions for which he first entered therapy to be helped to manage.

The patient has learned through years of experience that the most effective way to deal with a situation that cannot be managed effectively is to avoid it. It always works. It leads to other problems, deprivations, and unmet needs; but it still works. He/she can count on it. What the therapist is suggesting may or may not work, but avoidance always does. The patient forgets what the contract was with the therapist. He/she could not do the agreed upon exercise between sessions because visitors came from out of town. The images are no longer clear when systematic desensitization is practiced at home. In fact, the image can't be conjured up even in the therapist's office where, previously, this at least was possible. The patient or a member of his/her family have contracted the flu and so the next appointment is cancelled.

Rarely is the patient fully aware that these strategems serve the function of providing a reasonable basis for not entering the anxiety-evoking situation that he/she and the therapist have determined to be a goal of treatment. These cognitive strategies were often learned early as effective means of providing a rationale for irrational avoidance behavior. They constitute the cognitive part of a broad range of defensive strategies that also include affective and conative aspects.

The use of affect for avoidance or "defensive" purposes is evident when the patient responds to the endogenous, autonomic changes that accompany exposure to anxiety-arousing situations with exaggerated emotional reactions. Mild heart palpitations signal an imminent heart attack, which is reacted to catastrophically, so that leaving the scene becomes the only reasonable way to reduce the anxiety. More often, the endogenous source of the anxiety is not identified at all. Feeling anxious is followed by thoughts of "I'm losing control, I am dying," and more commonly, "I am going psychotic," which in a way provides the "ultimate" reason to avoid that situation on a subsequent occasion. When the patient's fear of going crazy has been reinforced by a previous therapist who was trained to believe that intense anxiety is always a sign of "ego" disorganization, there is even more justification for seeking immediate relief through withdrawal.

It is in the conative area, however, in the patient's structuring of interpersonal relationships and life conditions that the major defensive structures are evident. The patient's entire lifestyle often is designed with the avoidance theme constituting the major characteristic. The patient functions within a delimited range of love and work to assure the nonconfrontation of anxiety-evoking situations. In the social area, relationships may be few and friends chosen who make few, if any, demands and expect as little in return. Spouses are selected who are willing to provide continuous and uninterrupted emotional support, and who are "controllable"; jobs are gotten where challenges are below the capacities of the individual. The decision to go into therapy was arrived at with one major purpose in mind—to extend the network of supportive, nondemanding relationships to a professional who will especially be predisposed to providing continuous support, that is, relief from anxiety. It is the breakdown of the extant system of anxiety avoidance structures that brings the individual to treatment. This last point needs to be elaborated further.

Within the avoidance structure that the patient has constructed, he/she constantly moves between polar positions of fear of abandonment and fear of entrapment. This movement reflects early learned reactions to overcontrolling and nonsupportive parental figures. The fear of being entrapped in a relationship or in a job is counterbalanced by fear of abandonment, that is, rejection. The patient is, therefore, continuously moving toward or away from situations and individuals and maintains an uneasy precarious balance. Often the disequilibrium caused by an uncontrollable event makes the individual feel entrapped or abandoned, and precipitates a panic reaction that constitutes the precipitant for seeking treatment. The therapist is expected to make things right again; making things right is perceived to mean helping the patient move closer to the center of this bipolar region and reinstate the previous equilibrium. What is expected from the therapist is the reinforcement of avoidance maneuvers that are no longer working effectively. It does not mean confronting and dealing with the anxiety at either end of the abandonment-entrapment continuum. An understanding of this issue provides a conceptual basis on which the therapist may construct an effective strategy for dealing with resistance to change that, given the above considerations, is an inevitable feature of the treatment. This strategy must take the three aspects of resistance into account: the cognitive, the affective, and the conative.

The therapist, within the context of the therapeutic alliance, decides which approach to follow first in managing resistance when it occurs. It is often the cognitive track, as in psychodynamic therapy, that makes the most sense as the initial direction to go. The therapist interprets, or provides, cognitive inputs through which he attempts to get the patient moving again. He challenges directly the irrational assumptions and self-statements—that is, the belief system that patterns the patient's perception of the feared situation. Commitment to a lover, for example, may activate fears of being entrapped forever in a situation where one's basic needs, such as for autonomy and freedom of movement, will be frustrated. The dread that accompanies thoughts of a commitment was conditioned, of course, early in the life of the patient in relationships with parents where emotional closeness was indeed experienced as confining and punishing. The therapist encourages the patient to verbalize irrational thoughts and expectations and provides alternative rational inputs. This is done in a more structured manner than is the case in psychodynamic therapy, however. The cognitive restructuring techniques described by Meichenbaum (1977) and the interviewing methods described by Ellis (1962) are examples.

Cognitive restructuring techniques can be quite effective with some patients. Confronting resistance in this manner constitutes, of course, therapeutic change in and of itself and can free the patient to enter situations previously avoided. Much of the changes that occur in psychodynamic therapy are attributable to this cognitive change process.

In other patients, however, the fear of entering the situations they are avoiding is so intense that cognitive inputs prove to be ineffective. The anticipation of experiencing intense, uncontrollable anxiety in the situation mitigates against their attempting to enter into it and to learn appropriate ways of managing it. In these cases, methods for controlling anxiety, in general, such as "Benson's Relaxation Response" and anxiety specific to the target situation such as "systematic desensitization," are employed. Patients often are willing to undertake anxiety management training when it is suggested by the therapist because they are invested in the therapeutic relationship and so want to "give" something to the therapist. It also postpones the day when they will have to move out socially, get an apartment of their own, change jobs, get married, or whatever is the target behavior being addressed in the therapy. Relaxation training, when it is successful, provides the patient with a sense of control over anxiety that can allow him/her next to be exposed to the avoided situation in imagination. Systematic desensitization, "flooding," or some combination of these is then attempted. The maximum support of the therapist, at this point, may make the critical difference in the patient's willingness to risk this confrontation with the anxiety-evoking situation. The dimunition of anxiety through imaginal techniques may prove to be the sufficient next step in finally contracting with the patient to undertake entering a relationship, flying in a plane, having sexual relationships, enrolling in a graduate program, or whatever is the previously avoided behavior. The assumption here is made, of course, that the patient possesses the minimum necessary behavioral repertoire (i.e., skills, knowledge, intelligence, emotional resources) to indeed succeed at the proposed task. Higher levels of competence in the proposed target behaviors can then be acquired once the individual is able to freely enter the relevant situations.

Evoking resistance to confronting anxiety situations can be lessened significantly in some patients when the focus of treatment shifts to increasing the frequency and the quality of satisfactions they experience in their daily lives. Obviously, areas must be identified that constitute "conflict free" situations that the patient feels little or no anxiety in entering. These often include recreational activities like sports, music, and travel. Most individuals can identify some such situations that in the past were experienced as gratifying. (The therapist may assess what these may be by using a formal questionnaire such as in Lewinsohn's Life Satisfaction Inventory [Lewinsohn & Libet, 1972].) The patient is then encouraged in the sessions to enter these situations. Contracts are made when possible for the patient to attempt new things between weekly sessions.

This strategy can be extremely effective with some patients whose daily lives are characterized by a dearth of reinforcers. Adding more pain to their lives by setting up expectations to confront anxiety-evoking situations often constitutes the major source of their resistance.

There are other patients, however, with whom none of the cognitive and affective methods described above really work. They choose to dig in their heels and refuse to budge and the therapist senses that the treatment is on a downhill course and that an unsuccessful outcome is inevitable. The therapist is tempted to blame the patient and to resort to traditional diagnostic labels to explain to himself/herself why the treatment is not moving. A more thorough reexamination, instead of the social environment of the patient (that is, the contingencies that are maintaining his/her behavior in the course of his/her daily life), can prove more productive.

Resistance to change may be reinforced by individuals close to the patient who provide him/her with a continuous source of support, "negative reinforcement" if you will, that works against the motivation to take risks by confronting anxiety-evoking conditions. This process is best illustrated in cases of spouses who are always available to relieve patients' anxiety by insulating them from situations that stimulate it. It is clearly evident in cases of agoraphobic reactions where husbands are heavily invested in maintaining the symptoms of their wives. They are willing to go to great lengths at great personal sacrifice to assure that their wives never have to venture alone into situations that will arouse anxiety, such as driving a car or going to the supermarket. Parents of adult patients perform a similar function when they subtly discourage their sons and daughters from investing in relationships that could lead to personal commitments that will result in their separation. When this process begins early during childhood, it results in strong conditioned anxiety to separation in a broad range of situations. Employers serve a parallel function in not requiring from underpaid employees an output of work commensurate with their level of training and ability.

It is the accurate identification of these conditions that activate fears of separation or abandonment that occupies the clinical skill of the therapist. The insulating function of significant others is the interpersonal field of the patient's needs to be first understood. It is not always as clearcut an issue as the above examples might suggest. It becomes necessary, therefore, to include these complex variables in conceptualizing a strategy that finally is directed to altering the lifestyle of the patient in a manner that increases the probability of changing, in the process, the disordered behavior that is the presenting problem.

The most obvious one routinely attempted first is to include the significant other, or others, in the treatment sessions in the therapist's office. Clarification of the avoidance-maintaining function of the spouse or parent occupies the content of the sessions, as in traditional therapy. Contracts are then made by the therapist with the patient and the spouse or parent for the instigation of specific behavioral changes that will modify the maladaptive role functions of each of them. The presence of the therapist in this triadic structure provides that necessary condition or contingency for examining objectively what is going on between the two principals, and the "freedom," or sufficient anxiety reduction, for the patient to risk attempting to perform the previously inhibited behavior. When this succeeds, the therapist "reinforces" the patient with positive statements for the changes they effect from week to week.

A strong therapeutic alliance with the patient's cohort is a *sin qua non* condition for this strategy to work. The inevitable efforts to subvert the role-restructuring process by the cohort as well as the patient must be dealt with in these sessions. This is done through direct interpretations of why progress in implementing the behavior exchange contracts breaks down. It is critically important for the therapist not to limit his/her inputs to identifying the subversion tactics of one or the other partner, but principally to be "supporting" both in attempting to institute the new alternative behavior or lifestyle changes that are the therapeutic process at this juncture of the treatment. Often the entire social structural system in which the patient is currently functioning has been formed in a manner that will assure the reinforcement of a broad range of avoidance behaviors. Those significant others—spouses, bosses, and so forth—constitute only a part of this system. It also includes the occupation of the patient, his/her friendships, leisure activities, and life goals themselves. These other components of the patient's avoidance system need to be identified before specific techniques, such as assertion training, in relation to a significant other person can be productively employed.

A woman whose presenting problem is obesity, for example, may limit her close relationships to women. She chooses an occupation that has a high ratio of women to men, such as teaching. She is an active member of the feminist movement. Her mentor in graduate school is an unmarried woman. She maintains a close relationship to her mother and a weak one to her father. Her mother, in turn, centers her life on relationships to other women in the neighborhood in which she lives. The patient has acquired a lifelong pattern since puberty of overeating, that serves to effectively discourage approaches by men. To attempt to deal with obesity as a symptom independent of the social context in which this woman functions is to increase the probability of failure.

There are patients with whom none of the above strategies for dealing with "resistance" to change are effective. It becomes evident that their major goal in the sessions is to shape the therapist into providing them with the steady dosages of "support"—here translated as negative reinforcement they feel is needed to survive. They are often isolated individuals who rely heavily on the weekly sessions for nurturance and who feel that "moving out" to confront anxiety-evoking conditions, such as interpersonal relationships and more rewarding work, constitutes a direct threat to that dependent condition in which they are ensconced.

The therapist finds that he/she is a little more bored with the session and is drained at the end of the hour. The therapist begins to feel progressively more helpless and, indeed, longs to avoid the nonresponsive source of that feeling. A therapist may find himself/herself at that point without realizing how it came about. The patient seemed to be collaborating, after all. The arguments for not executing the contracts or getting into the desired new situations seemed reasonable. Much time was spent responding to the patient's protestations that they tried to do this or that, but it was impossible in spite of the anxiety management training or the support of their spouse or the fact that they have understood the irrational basis of their fears and employed cognitive restructuring techniques. The direct use of the therapeutic alliance itself as leverage for change may be considered as a strategy of last resort at this juncture. This can be effective only when the therapeutic alliance is a solid one. The patient has experienced the therapist as a strong ally who has the commitment and the expertise to help him or her. The patient values the relationship not only because of its negatively reinforcing function, but because at a cognitive level, at least, they "believe" that the therapist can in the end help them to overcome their problem or problems. The therapist announces that continued treatment by him/her is contingent on the patient's taking concrete steps in the planned directions. The reasons for this move on the therapist's part is explained in detail. The therapeutic relationship has become counter-productive for the patient, in the therapist's view. The therapist cannot, in good conscience, continue to serve a negative reinforcing function for the patient. A termination date is set. The patient is encouraged to participate in determining when the termination date might be. Often a minimum of two months is advocated by the therapist. The period is to be spent discussing the patient's feelings about termination. If, during that period, the patient feels ready to attempt to make concrete demonstrable changes consistent with the original treatment plan, the issue of termination can be postponed.

Patients react initially with disbelief to this posture of the therapist. They cannot believe a "paid" negative reinforcer could abandon them. The consequent anxiety is often sufficient to mobilize them in the direction of facing the anxiety-evoking conditions outside the therapy office which, until that point, they were successful in avoiding. Other patients choose to terminate. They will search for another therapist who will provide the necessary negative reinforcement interminably. Others consolidate those negatively reinforcing relationships with bosses, lovers, spouses, friends, and others, and will remain comfortable in these until a new crisis, activated by a disruption again of the abandonment-entrapment balance, will motivate them to return to the therapeutic situation. They might be careful to avoid a behavior therapist this time or they might actively seek one out depending on that balance of forces in their lives that determines their readiness to face the anxiety-evoking situations that have bound them.

The issue of "balance of forces" needs to be elaborated further. Much of what is labeled "resistance" often is attributable to a lack of appropriate identification of the complexity of the contingencies affecting the behavior of an individual. Effective behavior change is predicated on the therapist's correctly identifying where the patient is situated at a particular point in time in the context of those "events" that constitute the contingencies modifying his/her behavior (Spiegel, 1971). The therapist continually monitors what is happening in the life of the patient. What is happening includes such diverse events as physiological changes such as menstruation that occurs monthly, and middle-aging or menopause that occurs during a specific age period. It includes social events that occur infrequently, such as job changes, marriage, or death of a parent; and events such as inadequate sleep or lack of satisfying daily experiences that occur frequently. It also includes "cultural" events; that is, value changes in the society in which the individual now functions, that may constitute dramatic shifts from those in which he/she was socialized as a child. These cultural changes can result in frustration when the individual is unable to discriminate what constitutes appropriate behavior in different situations where previously learned responses no longer produce the intended effect. The current change in sexual mores is a case in point.

A critical parameter in this field of events that needs to be understood is

that referred to by transactional analysts as "life script." Through a myriad
of experiences during the early socialization process individuals acquire consistent perceptions of themselves and the course of life they will live in the
future. They "expect" their life will follow a particular course; these "expectations" modify their responses, (cognitive, affective, and conative) to conform with them. Often these expectations are not clearly in focus, out of the
awareness of the individual. Nonetheless, they constitute a modifying effect.

The patient's ability to move in the direction of changing target behaviors
may need to be postponed until these other contingencies are identified and
dealt with. Much of "dealing" with these contingencies involves the correct
clarification of their effect on the patient's behavior. Realizing that one's inability to achieve academically, for example, is caused by a fear that success
in this area will separate him/her from the love and support of a working
class, Italian family may be more important initially than desensitizing
him/her to the fear of studying (Papajohn & Spiegel, 1975). Intense anxiety
in the sexual area, for example, may be functionally related to the immediate
stimuli, i.e., approaches by members of the opposite sex or being alone with
such a person. The fear of disapproval learned in an early religious home environment, however, constitutes a critical contingency that needs to be dealt
with. Indeed, systematic desensitization to sexual anxiety may be "resisted"
since its successful completion will leave the patient exposed to the fear of
abandonment conditioned in the form of social disapproval and which continues to modify his/her behavior. In this example, it would be the fear of
social disapproval that would constitute the target behavior for desensitization. However, this "target" behavior in turn may be refractory to change
until the person's view of himself/herself in relation to sexual behavior is
clarified. The person may believe that truly "good" people are not sexual.
Sexual behavior is a characteristic of primitive people. This irrational view
may have to be addressed first at a cognitive level before focusing on desensitization at an affective level of either social disapproval or sexual behavior
itself. Furthermore, these irrational attitudes could be maintained by significant others in the current life of the individual with whom he/she has daily
contact. Behavioral engineering may involve encouraging the patient to expand his/her social interactions to include other individuals who can provide
"corrective" modifying experiences in the form of alternative, more reality
oriented, viewpoints. The patient can then be exposed to other people, in addition to the therapist who can model appropriate and, therefore, more effective behavior.

The posture of the behavior therapist in dealing with these complex contingency issues parallels that of his/her psychodynamically oriented counterpart in some ways, while in others it is dramatically different. The behavior
therapist facilitates through verbal inputs the clarification process and helps
the patient broaden his/her understanding of what is happening, i.e., what is

causing the distress. In doing so, the therapist is "supportive" and reinforces through positive statements the patient's efforts to identify what the relevant contingencies are that he/she is referring to. This process, however, is not the unstructured free associative kind that is reinforced in the psychodynamic therapies. The therapist assumes an active stance. He/she generates hypotheses as to what is happening and explores with the patient their validity. The patient is encouraged to formulate hypotheses of his/her own. The effort here again is task oriented and time limited. It is essentially a scientific enterprise undertaken by two people looking outward, not inward, for understanding.

By definition this clarification process precludes the concept of deep-seated pathology residing inside the patient which needs to be extirpated and neutralized through "insight." The focus is on interaction processes out there that caused (i.e., conditioned) in the past predictably consistent responses to current environmental events. An understanding of these complex processes is often necessary before intervention strategies can be effectively targeted on the appropriate behaviors.

It is a posture that generates "hope" in that the patient acquires a sense of the "rationality," or predictability, of events. Given a certain set of conditions one can predict certain outcomes. Given a punitive father and an overstrict religious background, one could predict an individual's hypersensitivity to criticism. Given a different set of conditions, such as the introduction of disinhibiting techniques and the assertive management of interpersonal relationships, one can predict a resolution to the presenting problem.

One's sense of helplessness in the face of confusing and seemingly unpredictable events is alleviated by this clarification of the cause and effect nature of experiences. The patient is told that indeed he/she can do something about these events and that he/she does have the ability to solve problems. When also equipped with the necessary techniques to effect this change, his/her sense of control is consolidated.

The tempo of the sessions themselves reinforces this sense of "hope" of moving toward a goal. Therapist and patient actively review what was accomplished in the week's period between sessions. The patient describes his/her efforts to enter anxiety-evoking situations, to increase the frequency and quality of gratifications in his/her life, to master assertive skills, and to effect control over his/her life by setting goals. The therapist teaches those skills required for the patient to progress in these directions—i.e., cognitive restructuring, anxiety management, goal setting behavior, and others. The therapist is maximally supportive of the patient in his/her efforts at change; however, support is contingent on effort invested and actual changes effected. The therapist also listens, knows when to let up, and is willing to empathize with the patient's pain. But all of these critically important, clinically sensitive responses of the therapist occur within a context of movement and change. This mood itself is not reinforcing of "resistance" maneuvers on the part of the patient. Indeed "resistance" will occur, but the mood and the tempo of the sessions mitigate against it. Patients will often attempt to neutralize this tempo by digging in and slowing down. They want to discuss feelings. The clinically sensitive therapist knows when this is a real need and responds empathetically. The therapist also senses when it is a maneuver to retard movement toward confrontation of anxiety-evoking conditions in patients' lives. The therapist may still pull back and ease off, although only temporarily. The therapist must constantly modulate the progress of the patient in order not to stress him/her to the point where the therapeutic effort becomes counterproductive. The patient feels overwhelmed and definitely wants out of the therapeutic situation that is making him/her feel more and more helpless and out of control—a "failure" in that expectations could not be met. This outcome can only occur when the therapist is characterized by a misunderstanding of learning principles, a lack of clinical skill, or both.

5

A Case History of a Person

with Agoraphobia

This case history was chosen because it illustrates the complex interaction of a series of events related to the onset and maintenance of multiple phobic symptoms in a 32-year-old woman. Her claustrophobic and agoraphobic symptoms were activated by identifiable situational variables in the present, i.e., enclosed places and open spaces. The onset of these phobic reactions, however, occurred at a point in time that was corollary to a separate event. Her husband undertook a new business venture that required his imminent absence from the home on business trips and also required her to work more in order to supplement the consequently diminished family income. She reacted with generalized anxiety and depression. Past events related to her symptoms were revealed in the behavioral analysis. Specific events were identified in experiences with significant figures during childhood, i.e., a favored teacher who had frequent and unpredictable epileptic seizures in class, the sudden death of her grandfather, and an episode when she was threatened sexually. General past events included her socialization in an extended ethnic home where she was, in her words, "overprotected," and where she was never allowed to be alone. Finally, her presenting phobic symptoms were intensified shortly after she completed her menstrual cycle. This "biological" event constituted an additional variable interacting with the social, situational and corollary events revealed in the behavioral analysis.

Mrs. Wilson was then a 32-year-old housewife living with her husband and three children in a middle-class suburb of Boston. She holds a bachelor degree in education from a teachers college, was brought up in a conservative Roman Catholic home, and is of Irish ancestry (her grandparents on both her mother and father's side being the original immigrants). She worked one day a week as a substitute teacher. Her husband, who is also a third generation Irish American, completed two years of college, and was a junior partner in a pharmaceutical supply company. Mrs. Wilson, an attractive light-complected woman, dressed stylishly but conservatively. Her husband, a tall and physically strong appearing person, is seven years older than his wife.

INITIAL INTERVIEW

Mrs. Wilson arrived 15 minutes early for her initial appointment accompanied by her nine-year-old son and seven-year-old daughter. She related easily, was articulate in expressing herself, while concomitantly she mediated apprehension through her body movements and the strained tone of her voice.

She thanked me for giving her an appointment so soon. She didn't know how much longer she could have lasted. She knew she had to see someone last month when she learned that a neighbor whom she knew only slightly committed suicide. She was overwhelmed with the dread that she too might lose control and kill herself. This dread took the form of persistent thoughts that she could not shake. At best, she feared, she might go crazy. (All of this in the first three minutes that she came into my office—her children waited on the other side of the door in the waiting room.)

She was also depressed, she said, because of these preoccupations and her inability to get rid of them. Was she a psychological cripple? Was she in fact going crazy? Her rate of speech had increased markedly over the last five minutes so that now it was quite rapid, although still articulate.

I listened attentively. I nonverbally communicated acceptance and I registered empathy through my body posture. I leaned over a bit to underscore my attentiveness. When I hear her ask me if I thought she was going crazy and she finally slowed down to signal she wanted a response from me, I complied with a reassuring statement: "I do not experience you as someone who is going crazy; anyone who feels very anxious, as you do now, will feel that maybe they are losing their minds, so to speak." I used this break, asked a series of questions—the beginnings of the formal behavioral analysis—questions focused on the present, on the precipitating events.

She had told me during our initial phone contact that she was referred by Dr. Cunningham, a behaviorally oriented psychiatrist. She went to him exactly a year earlier for help with her claustrophobia and agoraphobia. She did not use those terms. She described having terrible fears whenever she went out shopping, and whenever she found herself in enclosed places like church and the gymnasium where her nine-year-old son, a terrific athlete, played basketball. I asked her to be more specific.

She described the event that led her to see Dr. Cunningham. She had gone to shop at the local supermarket. Her three children were with her. She was in the checkout counter line. Suddenly, without any apparent reason, she began to feel intensely anxious. The intensity of her fear rapidly increased and it spread throughout her whole body. Her legs felt rubbery; she felt weak all over; she felt she was going to lose control, that is to say that she was going to faint, "pass out"; she was afraid she was going to die. Then the panic subsided by itself, also for no apparent reason. Shaken by the experience, she lived in fear that it would happen again. After that, she avoided checkout counters, supermarkets and markets of any kind, large buildings like churches and gymnasiums, bargain basements in large department stores, crowds, and any situation where she felt closed in and could not readily identify an exit. She also found (it was not clear to her the sequence in which she became fearful of situations) that she was afraid of driving long distances alone. Being alone was the most frightening situation of all and it was not clear to her how this symptom developed. She never went anywhere alone. Her husband was very helpful to her with her "problem," she said. He accommodated her whenever he could. He went with her to PTA meetings and basketball games at the local gymnasium and to church.

I inquired further about what else was happening prior to her going to see Dr. Cunningham. She, at this point, registered impatience with my questioning. She wanted to know what I could do for her to make this anxiety go away. How long would it take to make her better? She wanted to know when we were going to get started with the treatment. Did I plan to administer drugs to her as Dr. Cunningham had? I asked her to tell me about her treatments by Dr. Cunningham. Mrs. Wilson registered more impatience. She saw him for a total of six months. He had prescribed a drug, Tofranil, and suggested she not avoid going into situations that frightened her. He told her the drug would lessen her anxiety reactions and that gradually she would get used to going into these situations. The drug seemed to be working; she was definitely less anxious. Then she stopped taking the drug. I asked why and she responded that she didn't like taking drugs.

We were 35 minutes into the first session. Mrs. Wilson, as I mentioned above, talked very rapidly. I reaffirmed my understanding of her suffering. I began the reculturization process. I talked to her about learned anxiety reactions. They could be unlearned and I believed I could help her. I had to know more about what was causing her to be so anxious. She would have to bear with me until I could better identify with her what was setting off her anxiety reactions. So I began again to inquire about what was going on a year ago.

I learned that a month before she went to see Dr. Cunningham, her husband had announced he wanted to go into business for himself. This would put some financial strain on them for a while, but he hoped she could be patient. He also indicated he would be relying on her more for emotional support and he also intimated that it would be very helpful to him if she would be willing to work for more than one day a week. She found all of this very upsetting. The fact that he would want to rely so much on her for emotional support and to act as if it were her responsibility as to whether he were successful was especially disturbing.

At the end of the first session, Mrs. Wilson again asked directly as to whether I thought she was going crazy. I responded by saying I did not think so. She was markedly more relaxed. I felt I had begun to build a therapeutic alliance. I had the sense that I could help her. I saw no evidence of a thought disorder or other signs of behavioral disorganization of psychotic dimensions. I also knew she had been treated for a four-month period by a psychiatrist without manifesting any psychotic symptomatology. I felt confident in reassuring her she was not going crazy. Before she left I gave her the Fear Survey Schedule and the Life History questionnaire to be filled out for the next session.

SECOND SESSION

Mrs. Wilson came with her children again. She appeared markedly more relaxed. During the past week she reported feeling a bit less anxious. Anxiety still permeated her entire day, however, and she could not tolerate being alone. When her children went off to school and her husband to work she sought to spend the day with her mother who lived nearby, or girlfriends. I asked her to rate her anxiety that moment on a subjective scale of 0–100 with 100 marking the point of blind panic. She rated her anxiety at 70 degrees. I remarked that she didn't look that anxious—she assured me she was.

It was important, I told her, for us to trace back in her history the occurrence of extreme anxiety reactions so we could determine when and in what situations she had learned them. In order to help her unlearn them I needed to understand how she had acquired these anxiety reactions in the first place. There were techniques to alleviate her anxiety but they could be applied most effectively when the origins of these anxiety habits were better understood. My effort then was to pose focused questions inquiring into the past conditioning history of her phobic reactions. She caught on quickly and flooded me with information. When she was in high school she had a teacher whom she loved who was epileptic. This teacher would, without warning, have seizures in the middle of the classroom and have to be carried out bodily. Joan would be extremely upset and found that she worried continually about when the next seizure would occur. This teacher also taught Joan in the seventh and eighth grades in particular subjects, so that these experiences went on for a long time.

Then there was a girl in the fifth grade, who died of spinal meningitis. And there was a cousin who also had *petit mal* seizures that Joan knew about but had never witnessed.

When she was a senior in high school her grandfather became seriously ill and she was told he was not expected to live. During this period she remembered running to catch an elevated train on the way home from school. Her heart was beating fast from the physical exhaustion and then she remembered feeling suddenly very anxious; the anxiety came over her like a flood, she said, and built up to a crescendo. She was sure she was going to faint; she closed her eyes as if to prepare herself for passing out when just as suddenly the panic left her. But she was badly shaken.

Shortly after, she had a similar episode at her grandfather's funeral. She remembered walking toward his casket at the funeral home with the same panic engulfing her. She thought she was going to faint. After that experience she found she was afraid to go up in an elevator, and she was also afraid to go into other enclosed places. After she had been married for a year and was pregnant with her first child, her other grandfather died; again she experienced the same panic with a fear of "losing control" and fainting.

In recording this information (I took notes during the interview), my posture was one of empathetic listening punctuated with questions of clarification. These questions are posed in cause and effect terms and, of course, are designed to have the patient formulate her description of these events in specific behavioral terms rather than in abstractions. "What is it you mean when you say you felt you were going to faint? Can you remember what you were thinking just before you realized you were feeling anxious on the elevated train?" I asked. "That I'd be home soon and have to listen to my mother crying about her father, my grandfather, that is," she replied. "Were you reacting to your heart pounding?" "Yes, well it was like I became aware of my breathing and that my heart could stop, too," she answered.

The patient, toward the end of this second session, offered the following information that was not inquired into directly. A year back, shortly before she had decided she could not longer tolerate her anxiety and had sought help from Dr. Cunningham, she had had an experience which she had forgotten to tell me about. She had been on a marriage encounter weekend with her husband. She had initiated the idea of doing this because she felt her communication with her husband was not good. She'd hoped they could get closer. At one of the group meetings there were 26 couples in the same room and she began to feel closed in, then she panicked. I told myself I would inquire further into this event when, at a later point, I was able to take a more detailed history of her marital interactions.

In this session I wanted to broaden the behavioral analysis of past events to get an understanding of the emotional climate in which she grew up. Overprotectiveness emerged as the dominant theme. She elaborated this with many examples. Her mother was the dominant parent. She constantly worried about Joan and Joan's sister, who was older, and a younger brother. She worried about everything—that they were not dressed warmly enough, that something would happen to them on the way home from school. She was always very close emotionally to her mother and so was her sister. In fact, when her sister got married and moved to Indiana with her husband, her mother almost had a nervous breakdown. Her sister has since been divorced and is living in this area. Her younger brother, who was then 27 years old, had never married. He went out with women, but had never had a serious emotional relationship with one.

Mrs. Wilson seemed calmer by the end of this session and was able to verbalize this. She said her anxiety level was "about 40 s.u.d.s" (subjective units of disturbance). I anticipated her question, assuring her that in the next session I would teach her a technique to reduce her anxiety. She thanked me, and asked if I was sure it would work.

Two days after this session she called me to say she couldn't meet the following appointment; she said something about not being able to use the car that day. I told her it was important that she find a way. I was emphatic about this. It felt to me that she wanted to avoid the session. "Here comes the resistance," I thought, predictably after I had reassured her the previous session I would in fact "do something." I told her I expected her to come and emphasized the fact that my commitment to treating her was contingent on her coming at the appointed time. I felt this posture was important to a successful outcome. She came.

THIRD SESSION

I told her I would teach her a quick method of relaxing very deeply both physically and psychologically. A detailed explanation followed of the rationale undergirding this technique. I explained that this method induced physiological changes that were corollary to deep levels of physical rest and that these autonomic changes (I used that term) were inconsistent with, or antithetical, to anxiety. I asked her to close her eyes and repeat the word "one" subvocally and concomitant to exhalation. I stopped talking. In about ten minutes I instructed her to stop repeating the word "one," to keep her eyes closed for an additional minute (to "come out of it" gradually so that the autonomic balance could be reinstated). She reported feeling surprisingly relaxed. This statement reinforced my initial impression that this was the preferred relaxation technique for this patient. I instructed her to do it twice a day—before breakfast and dinner. During these two periods she was not to fight any anxious thoughts that came to her mind, while at the same time she was to bring herself back to intoning the word "one" when she became aware that she had been concentrating only on her anxious thoughts. She understood. Next I told her that at all other times during the day she was not to concentrate on anxious thoughts that come into her mind. A technique called "thought stopping" could be very helpful in this regard. I instructed her to close her eyes and to think an anxious thought. When she had this thought clearly in her mind and was feeling anxious because of it, she was to indicate this by raising her index finger. When she did so I shouted "stop." Yes, she said the thought was short-circuited. Now she was to repeat the same sequence, with the difference that she herself would shout "stop!" out loud when the anxious thought was clear and the accompanying anxiety was being felt. She did so. The third trial was the same except that I instructed her to shout subvocally. And that was all there was to it, I said. She should "thought stop" whenever anxious thoughts came in the normal course of the day. I alerted her to the fact that anxious thoughts might in fact increase in their rate of occurrence at the beginning, but that she was to persevere. She asked me several questions, most of them elicitations of assurance that the techniques would work. I told her if they didn't I had others we would try next. I felt, however, there was a good chance that these two particular ones were well suited to help with her problem. Besides these were only preliminary efforts we were making to provide her with some relief from her anxiety. We would be employing other methods to unhook her anxiety reactions from those stimuli that elicited them. I meant, I quickly added, those situations that activated them (like the checkout line at the supermarket).

In this session I also spent time elaborating the point that it was her current habit of never going alone anywhere that reinforced or maintained her anxiety symptoms. It was important for her to consider it was exposure to those situations that would result in a therapeutic outcome. It was my intention to work out methods for her to be exposed in a systematic way to situations that now made her anxious so she could begin to get "used to" going into them alone. I suggested we start by agreeing to come to the next session alone. It was surprising to me that she agreed rather easily to contract with me to leave her children at home next session. She understood the rationale of my explanation and was willing to cooperate.

In summary, then, this third session was focused on meeting different objectives. First was the continued reinforcement of the therapeutic alliance. My empathetic response to her throughout the session was in itself anxiety-reducing because of the support she felt by my interest in and concern with her problem. Secondly, I provided her with specific techniques to reduce her anxiety. Thirdly, I provided cognitive inputs in the form of explanations of her anxiety as a learned reaction and the concept of exposure as a process through which it could be unlearned. Finally, I initiated an *in vivo* flooding procedure by getting her to agree to come in alone the next time. An additional advantage derived from teaching her Benson's Relaxation Response was that it provided her with a method of relaxing that I intended to incorporate into a desensitization program at a later point in the treatment.

FOURTH SESSION

Mrs. Wilson came alone to this session. She reported right off that she was surprised that she was not anxious while driving to my office alone. Furthermore, her anxiety level during the past week was quite low, on the order of 20 s.u.d.'s. The technique I taught her, she said with a surprised look on her face, seemed to be working. She had practiced Benson's Relaxation Response twice a day, before breakfast and late in the afternoon, faithfully, and it had a definite effect. The "thought stopping" also worked well; it was such a relief not to have to be preoccupied with those anxious thoughts all day.

I felt I could proceed now to preparing the patient for systematic desensitization. The first step was to do a functional analysis of the situations that activated phobic reactions in her current daily life. I proceeded to obtain detailed behavioral descriptions of when she became anxious, under what conditions, and with what degree of intensity. My objective was to identify as many of the pertinent variables as possible in these situations.

The following situations were isolated as being both current and highly troublesome to the patient:

1. Standing in a long line at the checkout counter in a crowded supermarket.
2. Sitting in the viewer stands at an athletic complex watching her son play basketball.
3. Standing in a large indoor open space like an auditorium.
4. Walking alone along the street in downtown Boston, mingling with crowds of people—even with someone. (She said would be impossible alone.)
5. Sitting in a dentist's chair having her teeth fixed.
6. Sitting at a table in a center of a restaurant (even with other people).
7. Sitting in church, in the center of a pew which in turn is in the center row. (Access to exits is, therefore, difficult.)
8. Sitting at a table at a particular girlfriend's house (feeling hemmed in by the close quarters).
9. Finding herself in a bowling alley and being expected to bowl.
10. Finding herself totally alone during the day (with no access to her husband, parents or others).

Those situations became the foci of therapeutic change. The next objective became that of disassociating anxiety responses from the stimuli operative in these specific conditions of the patient's life. The approach to effecting this disassociation or unlearning was to be twofold, i.e., *in vitro* and *in vivo* (in imagination and in the real life situations concurrently). The rationale undergirding the technique of systematic desensitiation was explained to the patient in detail. She would learn to be relaxed in these situations first through reconstructing the conditions in imagination and substituting a relaxation response for the anxiety reactions she was now experiencing. When her anxiety was sufficiently reduced in imagination she would enter into the real situation itself. It would be expected that after systematic desensitization her anxiety in these situations would be of a low degree of intensity. Entering these situations repeatedly in the real world would eventually result in the complete diminution of the anxiety reaction.

Mrs. Wilson did not look very convinced. I reassured her. We would go slowly and first take the least anxiety-provoking situation from her list (watching her son play basketball in the open athletic complex) and save the most anxiety-provoking (being alone all day) for last.

Mrs. Wilson said that perhaps we ought to postpone this procedure for a while. It made her anxious just thinking about it. I reminded her that we would be doing the procedure first in imagination and that she would probably feel more confident about actually going into these situations after she had been desensitized in this manner. The next session I would teach her how to imagine scenes representing the anxiety-evoking situations she had described today. In the meantime she was to continue doing Benson's Relaxation Response and also to use thought stopping when necessary.

FIFTH SESSION

Mrs. Wilson reported that she continued feeling less anxious throughout the day. She continued to avoid situations, however, that could make her anxious and she also avoided going places alone. Coming to my office was the exception; in fact, it was even easier doing so this week than the previous week.

The major focus of this session was on imaginal training and on training in the procedure of systematic desensitization itself. I asked Mrs. Wilson to close her eyes and imagine herself in an emotionally neutral situation, such as sitting at home drinking coffee with her husband. I instructed her to construct this scene piecemeal in her mind. She was to focus sequentially on the different aspects of this scene and to include all relevant sensory modalities. She was to identify the furniture in her breakfast nook in her house, the contour of the table, the color of the curtains, and other items. She was to focus on the look on her husband's face, the sound of the spoons hitting the coffee cups, the taste and feel of the coffee as she drank it, and the feeling of the chair beneath her. Also, she was to imagine the feel of the bathrobe she was wearing, and other items. I asked her periodically to rate the degree to which she felt she was really in that situation on a scale of one to five, with five indicating the best fit to the real situation. It took about three tries with three emotionally neutral scenes before she was able to construct one that she could rate a four for its clarity and "realness."

I next decided to move to the construction of a scene from among those situations she had previously described as anxiety-provoking. We decided to begin with a situation that was both low in its anxiety-evoking potential and current because she would be confronted with having to enter it during the following week. (It had to be current if we were to include the *in vivo* component of desensitization program in this first try.) I instructed her to close her eyes and imagine herself sitting on the hard seats in the spectators' section of the large gymnasium where her son played basketball. "First, actually try to feel the seat beneath you; focus on the lights coming in through the large windows at either end of the gymnasium," I told her. "Now focus on the movement of the boys running back and forth on the court. Now single out your own son and notice his characteristic way of moving his body. Now concentrate on the color of the opposing team's uniform. If at any time throughout these instructions you begin to feel anxious, indicate by raising your forefinger. Okay, now shift your eyes to a panoramic view of the entire gymnasium. . . ." Mrs. Wilson's finger shot up. "Okay, hold that scene." I hold her fixed in that scene for five seconds and then instruct her to "shut out the scene, clear your mind, relax."

It was clear the procedure was working. The imagined scene evoked anxiety. I asked her to shut it off relatively soon because I wanted to gauge how much anxiety (on a scale of 0–100) was being elicited by the scene. I didn't want to flood her with anxiety in this procedure. I wanted to modulate the degree of anxiety she was exposed to so that it would not exceed 30 or 40 s.u.d.s.

While her eyes were still closed, I asked her how much anxiety she had experienced while she was exposed to the scene. She said, "about 45 degrees." I expected this scene to be relatively less anxiety-provoking than others we had explored in the previous session because she had delegated the real life situation that is represented to the lowest position on the hierarchically ordered list she had compiled.

Next, I instructed her to relax very deeply using Benson's Relaxation Response Method. When she was absolutely relaxed and she could rate her anxiety at below 20 degrees, she was to indicate by raising her forefinger. When she did so I asked her to turn on the gymnasium scene again. When she again felt anxious she was to indicate by raising her forefinger. When she did so I began timing and on this trial I lengthened her exposure to the anxiety evoked by the scene to 15 seconds.

"Okay, shut off the scene, clear your mind and relax very deeply again," I said. "When you are totally relaxed, indicate by signaling me a second time." When she did so I asked her how much anxiety on a scale of 0–100 she experienced that time. She told me it was about the same, although probably a bit higher that time.

I repeated this procedure for the next 25 minutes in the office. We were able to complete about 15 trials—at the end of which her anxiety had been reduced to about 25 s.u.d.s.

I contracted with her to set aside two half-hour sessions each day immediately following the 20 minutes she did Benson's Relaxation Response in order to practice this technique. Estimating a minimum of 15 trials each session, she was expected to complete 150 trials in the five-day period that preceded the day she was to attend a basketball game her son was playing in at the local school gymnasium. The *in vitro* desensitization she had gone through was to prepare her to enter into the real situation at that time. She was to call me on the phone if her anxiety was still so high on the day that she felt she could not do it. Otherwise, she should go to the game, since it was through exposing herself to the real situation that the desensitization would be completed.

THE NEXT EIGHT SESSIONS

Mrs. Wilson reported to me at the next session, which was her sixth, that the procedure worked for her and that her anxiety had been reduced sufficiently enough by the systematic desensitization for her to be able to risk going to the basketball game. Once there, she was a bit uneasy at first because she still expected her anxiety might rise suddenly and get out of control—but it didn't. As the time passed, she became more reassured; for a while she was actually able to forget about her anxiety and "lose herself" in the game.

In these next eight sessions Mrs. Wilson and I worked through the hierarchy of anxiety situations that she had described earlier during the functional analysis. We followed the same procedure of paralleling *in vitro* (in imagination) desensitization with *in vivo* exposure to the real situations. We moved through the hierarchically ordered list of situations, from least to most anxiety-evoking. Each of these sessions began with my asking her at the onset how it went with the particular situations we were working on that week. In other words, the session was structured in a manner whereby I set up the expectation, or provided the external control, to increase the probability that she would carry out the contract we had agreed upon the previous time. This contract, of course, included both doing the desensitization exercises at home (and also continuing Benson's Relaxation Response and thought stopping), and entering into the real situations themselves. This "structure" I provided was not sufficient, however, to keep Mrs. Wilson from engaging in a whole repertoire of avoidance behaviors. These avoidance behaviors (resistance) increased in frequency and complexity as Mrs. Wilson proceeded in expanding the range of previously claustrophobic and agoraphobic situations she was able to enter into successfully. After a couple of successful experiences (standing in the checkout counter at the supermarket and eating in a restaurant at a centrally located table), Mrs. Wilson reported that she was having trouble finding time to do the desensitization exercises. Then she reported that Benson's Relaxation Response was no longer working; in fact, it made her more anxious because it increased her feeling of losing control. On three occasions, she called to cancel the next appointment. I held firm and she came. I also took a firm, but supportive, posture in dealing with the other "resistance" issues. I expected her to do the exercises; I couldn't help her if she couldn't find time. I gave in, however, on Benson's Relaxation Response. She could postpone doing it for the time being.

During these eight sessions, when rapid therapeutic changes were taking place, a considerable portion of the 50 minutes were devoted to exploring with Mrs. Wilson the thoughts and feelings she was experiencing between sessions. Mrs. Wilson felt frightened, she said, by her feelings. When I inquired further she said she felt at times she might be overwhelmed by her anxiety and lose control. These feelings were not immediately connected by her to entering previously phobic situations. They came at other times during the day. That's why she didn't like doing Benson's Relaxation Response. She had a dream. A man catches her in an abandoned warehouse, strips her, and says, "This time I'll let you go but next time. . . . " This dream triggers off a memory of an experience she had at the age of nine or ten. She was walking home from school when she was approached by six or seven black children who pushed her against a wall, but didn't harm her; she ran home in a panic state.

I reassured Mrs. Wilson about her intense anxiety. No, she was not going crazy. The intense feelings of anxiety are probably precipitated, I told her, by the fact she was doing things she hadn't done in a long time and going into situations she had avoided in the past. Her anxiety would subside. It did.

I explored her sexual dream and specifically the possible connection between sexual feelings and "exposure" in open places or being "caught" in claustrophobic situations. This line of inquiry led nowhere. She began to wonder about my preoccupation with sex. The next major issue she brought up was a physical one. She was having excessive vaginal bleeding after her last period. She called her gynecologist but he was on vacation so she would not be able to have it checked for another six weeks; she was sure she had cancer. Why didn't she go to another gynecologist? She wanted to wait for Dr. McCarthy to come back. The following week she reported the bleeding had stopped. She felt less anxious but still apprehensive. I urged her to see another doctor—she held firm. No mention again was made of this problem. (When her own Dr. McCarthy finally saw her the bleeding had stopped completely and all tests he did, including a Pap smear, were negative.)

In the eleventh session Mrs. Wilson reported that she felt so good that she was sure something bad was going to happen. She often found, she said, that when she realized during the course of the day she is getting better that she is tempted to bring on that feeling of anxiety again. I told her not to.

The other theme that emerged during these last eight sessions was her relationship with her husband. As she got better she talked about it more and in greater detail. She was very angry at him and had been for years. It started about two years after they were married; he would stay out late every Friday, playing cards and gambling with his friends. He would lose money they didn't have. She'd wait up for him all night, getting more furious with the passage of each hour. He would finally come home. She felt like killing him. He'd go right to bed and fall asleep. He no longer gambled; but she was still angry at him and he wouldn't let her express it. He shut her out, or got furious at her if she raised questions about what he was doing. She realized that this was part of the marriage contract—he would protect her, she would obey. She didn't want it this way anymore—especially since she was feeling so good lately (that is, free from anxiety).

By the thirteenth session the patient was relatively symptom free. She shopped in supermarkets, went to restaurants, and could be alone in her car. She was not apprehensive when her husband went away on a business trip. Her gynecological problems abated. She no longer felt apprehensive during the day and her bad dreams ceased.

There were still periods, however, when she felt the old fears coming back (Mrs. Wilson was by then a good behavioral analyst), particularly after she had an argument with her husband. It was this idea he has of going into business for himself; it was like gambling, in a way. After all the years they'd struggled to get on their feet financially, and he wanted to risk it all on this new venture. He wanted her to work more days as a substitute teacher to get him through this period; besides, this new venture would force him to travel frequently and be absent from the home.

The preliminary aspects of the therapy were by then finished. The patient's phobic symptoms were sufficiently alleviated through the use of systematic desensitization and exposure to the real situations to warrant undertaking the second major aspect of the therapy—the patient's interaction with her social environment. In Mrs. Wilson's case, this involved changing her mode of interaction with her husband in more assertive directions and, secondly, acquiring more independent modes of relating to the world in general. The latter approach involved learning to cope with progressively larger amounts of life activities as an individual, independent from the support she was getting from her husband and other significant people in her life—including her therapist. In this direction, I planned to instigate changes in the work and nonwork situations. The gains she made so far could not be maintained unless lifestyle changes in these two major areas were affected. A critical aspect of this instigational aspect of therapy was her relationship to me. It was clear, of course, that she had generalized (transferred, if you prefer) her learned habit of reducing anxiety through support from strong parental figures from her husband to me. I expected that termination of treatment at this point, without the lifestyle changes described above, could have resulted in an exacerbation of symptoms. (It did anyway at the end of treatment, but the recurrence of her symptoms was temporary. I will discuss this issue later.) In other words, she had to have the experience of dealing with the world effectively through her own efforts before her fears of being contained, on the one hand (claustrophobia), and being abandoned on the other (agoraphobia), would finally and completely be alleviated.

THE NEXT THREE MONTHS

The focus during the next 12 sessions shifted to her marital relationships, on the one hand, and her lifestyle, specifically work activities and "other" activities, on the other hand. The "other" category included but was not limited to, leisure time activities. However, I continued to monitor in the first few minutes of each session her activities of the previous week that were related to maintaining her therapeutic gains. This monitoring included my urging her to enter new situations previously avoided, when the opportunity afforded itself from week to week. New situations not included specifically in her original list were added. (She shopped by herself in the basement of a large Boston department store, Filene's; she accompanied her husband to a large, yearly social function given by his company which in previous years she had avoided.) She now "desensitized," as she called it, to these new situations before she entered them as a matter of course.

I first concentrated in two sessions on orienting her cognitively to taking an assertive, not aggressive, stand toward her husband. I reviewed the rationale undergirding this technique, did some role playing in the office, and arranged for her husband to come in the third session after we had entered this phase. He came reluctantly to the first session. He was very angry at me. What did I think I was doing? His wife had become progressively more difficult to deal with.

I concentrated on both establishing a therapeutic alliance with the husband and making him aware of his authoritarian role in the marital relationship. I underscored the two-way aspect of the issue; she wanted him to protect her in the past but now she wanted to renegotiate their marital contract. I pointed out the benefits to be gained from this shift and also pointed out what the losses would be. He had to be very careful not to be shaped by her into supporting her dependency on him by accompanying her to different places. He had no idea that she was experiencing so much anxiety in the past. She said he never let her talk about it to him, that's why he had no idea. He said he needed her help since he had, indeed, decided definitely to start his own company. She said that this made her very anxious. I suggested she work more than one day a week. I explained the psychological importance to her of moving out and learning to deal with stresses in the work-a-day world; besides, it would reinforce her husband emotionally and provide an important source of revenue that they needed. She refused adamantly to increase her work load. Whose side was I on anyway?

I explored other activities Mrs. Wilson might consider for her leisure time besides visiting her mother or spending time with close girlfriends. This too proved to be a difficult area. I allied myself again with her husband in considering ways she might be more productive in her leisure time. She spontaneously offered to help her husband with his work; she would take on some of the secretarial tasks involved. She finally agreed to work one more day a week substitute teaching. She resumed painting, which she had done during college. She took a more active role in the local P.T.A. She joined the woman's auxiliary of her local church. She took an active role in planning family vacations. She found she could tolerate her husband's absences on business trips with little or no anxiety.

Mrs. Wilson learned to be appropriately assertive with her husband, and he responded to her assertive behavior in appropriate ways. Their communication improved markedly. Each week we took up the issues going on between them in the previous week. My posture remained that of the third party intervener, or consultant, providing expert advice on improving their relationship and also searching for new areas where Mrs. Wilson could practice independent, assertive behaviors. We were nearing the end of this phase after 25 weeks into the treatment. I suggested we set a termination date. Also, I suggested meeting alone with Mrs. Wilson for the remainder of the sessions.

THE TERMINATION PHASE

I expected the termination phase to be a difficult period for Mrs. Wilson, but hadn't anticipated the intensity of her reaction. The week after I had raised the issue of termination she reported a complete exacerbation of all her symptoms. She said she was just as bad, if not worse, than when she first came in. All her phobias had returned, *"all of them."* She could hardly get up the nerve to leave her house and drive to my office. She moved back to substitute teaching one day a week. She actually succeeded in manipulating her husband to drive her to the local school to vote in the state elections; and she informed me with some relish that she made sure he waited outside the voting booth so she could see him the moment she stepped out of it.

I was supportive and said something like terminating treatment was difficult. I suggested the following plan: we would agree on a termination date four weeks hence; then I would see her once a month for the next three months and after that, three months for the last time. She agreed. During the next four weeks her therapeutic gains were reinstated. I spent these sessions recontracting for her to go into situations she was again avoiding. I did the same thing during the three monthly sessions. The last session was uneventful. She had already made the break. It was a boring session for both of us; she could hardly wait for it to end.

I called up Mrs. Wilson six months later. She had maintained her gains, she informed me somewhat reluctantly. When I phoned again six months after that (a year since our last session), Mrs. Wilson was pleasant, but impatient, with me. I was clearly keeping her from doing things.

6

A Case History of a Person with

Obsessive Ruminations

This patient, then a 21-year-old male college junior, initially presented that configuration of behaviors referred to in the psychodynamic literature as the "obsessive-compulsive personality." His reaction to stressful situations was characterized by obsessive thoughts of catastrophic outcomes with preoccupations of personal failure and rejection comprising the corollary theme. This disorder of thinking was analyzed behaviorally in terms of those past and present environmental contingencies that shaped and maintained it. The psychological, social, and cultural events that inhibited him from "moving out" psychologically and socially intensified his unconditioned fear of entrapment and abandonment. His ambivalence in relationships with women constituted the major locus of his fears of abandonment on the one hand and engulfment on the other hand. The conditions of his early life, mainly the relationship with his parents, mitigated against his acquiring the necessary interpersonal skills with women that could lead to emotionally satisfying relationships. The treatment strategy that evolved was directed to helping him manage his anxiety as he moved toward effecting those lifestyle changes that freed him to satisfy his needs for emotional closeness and to reinforce his sense of control over the other events of his life.

Paul Cohen was working as an attendant in the mental hospital serving the small midwest community where he lived. This was the summer between his sophomore and junior college years. He had been working long hours, primarily the night shift, and was very tired. He was living at home but hadn't seen his parents who were on an extended vacation for several weeks; his younger brother was away at camp. He was about to leave the hospital for home—it was early in the morning—when a young man whom he knew from high school days was admitted to the emergency unit of the hospital. He was floridly psychotic. He was smiling inappropriately and making obscene gestures at the staff. The policeman who brought him in said that among other things the patient was a known homosexual.

Paul felt a dread start to engulf him as he aided the psychiatrist who was talking to the young man and preparing to administer medication intravenously. His intense anxiety was accompanied by thoughts that he, too, might be a homosexual and that he might become insane. These preoccupations had a persistent repetitive quality. However, he managed to control himself sufficiently so that he got through the remaining intake procedure assisting the psychiatrist. His anxiety subsided considerably when he got home and although he was quite tense he managed to fall asleep. He awoke with anxiety the next day, but this intensity was much less and the preoccupations more fleeting than persistent. He decided to skip work that night. The next day he felt practically "normal" again, although still apprehensive that he might get another "attack." He shared his experience and his concern with a psychologist on the staff, who suggested he find himself a therapist. Paul also decided not to finish out his last two weeks at the hospital before he returned to college. The week he got back he sought out a counselor at the mental health center of the college, who saw him for a single evaluation session. This counselor decided that he was in need of intensive treatment by a private therapist and referred Paul to me. The referring counselor also felt that Paul was not particularly open to "insight" therapy, needed a strong male figure to "identify" with, and an experienced therapist to help him manage the intense anxiety to which he was vulnerable.

THE INITIAL INTERVIEW

Paul appeared as a lean, tall man with long sandy colored hair, a beard that was not particularly well-groomed, and steel rimmed glasses; the combination conveyed the impression of a liberated counterculture college person. The impression that emerged in this session was not consistent with the realities of his lifestyle.

He related the previous summer's incident at the mental hospital and stated that his purpose for seeking help was the fear that his panic might recur. In fact, just two weeks ago he had a fight with a girl he was dating and began to feel tense and anxious; as a result he started to be preoccupied with the fear he might have another episode.

Paul showed no outward signs of tension and anxiety during this session. There was an abstract, intellectual cast to his formulations of the events in his life that brought him to my office. It was as if he were talking about someone else, doing a clinical analysis of some other patient, as he responded to my inquiries. In fact, he needed little input from me in focusing on the areas that were relevant to the behavioral analysis I was undertaking. I knew he was tuned into what I wanted to learn about, so I made no effort to be systematic by exploring the presenting problem first and the broader, horizontal, historical track later. Both areas were covered comprehensively by him in this and subsequent sessions comprising the early phase of treatment.

He is one of two children of Jewish parents. His brother, five years younger than he, was not a particularly good student in the high school he was attending in his home town. He grew up in a "WASPY" community in a small town; his family was only one of about a dozen Jewish families in the whole city. His father owned a large clothing store in the town and did quite well. He had had aspirations to go to college, but abandoned them because his parents were poor. His mother was very bright but she, too, was only a high school graduate. His mother helps his father with the clothing store and they get along well with each other. His father tends to overreact to stressful situations by getting very emotional. Paul remembered this happening as a child when business was not going well. His father would tell them he was on the verge of bankruptcy and to be prepared for the hard times were ahead. His mother tends to be emotional also, but less so. He always had a good relationship with both his parents, can discuss issues openly with them, and had always experienced them as supportive.

His childhood was colored by two central events. The first was his isolation from his peer group when he was growing up. This goes back as far as he can remember—most prominently in grammar school and less so in high school. He was discriminated against by the neighborhood kids because he was a Jew. They called him anti-Semitic names and made life difficult for him. He spent long summers by himself at home. In high school he was an excellent student, got a lot of approval from his teachers, dated some of the girls, and felt much less isolated.

The second traumatic event he remembered vividly was the birth of his younger brother. He was around five, and felt that his mother had abandoned him; it was an awful feeling. He started bed wetting. He remembers his mother changing him; it felt good to have her full attention again. He still does not get along well with his brother.

He had a lot of trouble separating from his parents as he was growing up. The one attempt to go to camp when he was ten ended badly; he had to leave and go home after a week because of intense feelings of loneliness. During high school he went away for a week to another city to take a special honors type course and he was miserable. He had trouble relating to the other students. They were more sophisticated than he and had traveled a great deal with their parents.

When he first learned of his acceptance to the very prestigious university he now attends, he experienced a short period of panic, but then quickly recovered. The approval he received from everyone helped to neutralize his anxiety. Furthermore, knowing he could not avoid going (his parents were ecstatic at his good fortune of being accepted) tended to lessen his anxiety. His adjustment at college was on the whole surprisingly easy. From the very first day he arrived, he made friends with other Jewish men in the freshman class and eventually shared a room with two of them. He called home frequently at first, but less so after a while. His friendships with male friends were good and lasting, but his relationships with girls were problematic from the beginning. He had intercourse with a girl for the first time a month and a half before he started treatment with me. He was currently going out with two different girls—both Jewish. He was, he thought, in love with the first, Nan, and was having sexual relations with the second, Sue.

In this initial session I listened, and was supportive and reassuring. I began the reculturization process by specifically elaborating the notion of anxiety as a learned response which could be unlearned. I felt a rapport with him. I told him we could focus more on his relationship to Nan and Sue in the second session.

THE NEXT NINE SESSIONS

The next nine sessions, from the second week in October until the first week in February, constituted the first distinct phase of the therapy with Paul Cohen. It was not planned that way by me. He decided to terminate after the tenth session and he resumed treatment three weeks after that because of a crisis that had occurred in his life. The second phase of the treatment, which began at the end of February and ended in the middle of the following December, was markedly different from the first. I saw Paul for a total of 36 sessions over a 13-month period.

In the second through the tenth sessions of the first phase of treatment, various objectives were met. The behavioral analysis was first of all expanded and events raised in the first session were elaborated in greater detail. The reculturization process was reinforced by continual inputs from me in which the events he related to me were fed back to him in behavioral, "cause and effect" terms. He focused a great deal on the relationship to the two women he was involved with and the eventually unsuccessful effort was made to clarify the source of his anxiety about each of them. Efforts by me to implement a structured treatment intervention strategy with systematic desensitization as a major technique never got off the ground. Clearly Paul got relief from the anxiety he brought with him to the initial session through talking to a sympathetic therapist; but, as it subsequently emerged, this gain, too, was short-lived. I was concerned about developing a therapeutic alliance with him; but he experienced our relationship as one in which he was becoming increasingly more dependent on me and this, he told me, was aversive to him. Also, he said he was afraid of uncovering events in his life that would make him anxious; this would interfere with his school work and so he could not afford to remain in treatment. My response to this latter issue, namely that the major focus of the treatment would be in dealing with current issues rather than childhood events, seemed at the moment not to make any impact on him. He was not taking any chances that he might be exposed to associations that could activate the anxiety he dreaded and which he now had under control. Three weeks after he had broken off his session with me, he terminated his relationship with both Nan and Sue; this event precipitated the anxiety reaction that brought him back into treatment for the second time.

The major issues covered and the trends that evolved in the remainder of the nine sessions of the first phase of the treatment will be summarized next.

Paul elaborated on the circumstances of his panic reaction in the mental hospital the previous summer. He had been feeling quite alone for several days before it happened. His parents were away and he was also isolated from his friends back east who were students with him at the university. He had also developed some friendships lately in his home town with college men who also had returned home to work for the summer, and he could not see them either because he worked the night shift at the hospital. He had felt the tension rising and he felt sorry for himself and very angry at his parents. He also had trouble sleeping and so was very fatigued during his waking hours. He was also preoccupied that summer with one major issue in his life—his inability to form a close emotional relationship to a girl. He had tried the previous spring at college and had failed. He had gone out with girls, but was never close emotionally or sexually. Maybe, he thought to himself, he was a "faggot." When that young man was admitted to the hospital the uncontrollable fear that he would end up the same way welled up in him.

The fear of insanity, he said, was caused in part by the fact that his maternal grandmother had spent most of her life in a mental hospital and his first cousin on his mother's side had been hospitalized for a year with a serious emotional illness.

The intensification of his efforts to form a relationship with a woman after he got back to college in the fall was related to his fear of being a homosexual and of "going crazy." It was easy to get into a sexual situation with Sue. No, he did not feel anxious when he approached her or during the sexual act itself, in spite of the fact it was his first time with a woman. He did not care about her; he was not emotionally close to her. "Maybe that was why," he thought out loud. With Nan, however, it was another matter. He was "in love" with her, but she was going out with another student and declined to have sex with him. They petted and "stuff like that" but no sex. He was very depressed by this and worked very hard at trying to get her to give up this other man. When she appeared to be leaning in the direction of doing so, he found she became less appealing to him. He proceeded to relate to me her many faults (until that point he had been unaware of them). I pointed out to him that it looked as if it was very frightening for him to be in a situation with a girl who was willing to be committed to him, and that he also liked, because it could result in a kind of bond that would have a confining, entrapped feeling. He said he could not see this. He did not feel particularly anxious when she indicated a willingness to leave her boyfriend. He just wasn't as sure that he wanted to limit his relationship with women to one person only; besides, she was a very shallow person. It was clear I was not making much headway in the direction of clarifying this issue with him at this point in treatment. I understood, then, what the referring psychologist meant when she said he wasn't open to insight therapy. That she and I were both wrong about this point became evident in the course of the second phase of treatment.

The third major issue that he brought to me during his initial phase of treatment was his fear of disapproval. It originated, he said, in his relationship with his father. He gets very anxious at the thought of disapproval by his father or by any of his professors at college. He is a straight "A" student and is majoring in sociology, although he has had thoughts about applying to a graduate program in business administration.

I suggested that the fear of rejection was also an issue with girls and because it preoccupied him so much we ought to consider doing something about it therapeutically. I thought this could be a start for a more focused deconditioning program to supplement the desensitization that was going on in the interpersonal interaction between us during the therapy hour. He agreed. We tried it. We constructed scenes from actual life events in which he had experienced anxiety about rejection. The figures in these scenes were authority figures such as professors, bosses, and so forth. It didn't work. He couldn't keep the images clear; the anxiety they aroused was minimal and besides it was clear he wanted to talk. So I abandoned the procedure. I also felt that while indeed he was an obsessive person the sessions were not ones where obsessive and nonproductive ruminations were consuming the therapeutic hours. Nor did I feel that he was in the process of attempting to induct me into an extant system of dependent relationships that he had with others. I felt that, quite the opposite, he was already embarked on an effort to free himself from the constraints of a system of dependent relationships, principally with his parents. He had begun to move out toward individuating himself by contracting relationships with women and confronting the anxiety activated by male authority figures. The episode of last summer marked the critical move outward toward separating himself from the security of a dependent relationship with parents and toward an independent, adult, "emotional" relationship with a woman. And so I listened and supported him because he was confronting anxiety through sharing these critical life experiences with me, which is the essence of the therapeutic process. To think in terms of "mechanisms of defense" at this juncture is to obscure one positive, therapeutic outcome that was part of his experience of pervasive anxiety. My job was *not* to "shore up his defenses" but to modulate his exposure to anxiety in a manner that assured its gradual desensitization. I looked for openings to facilitate this "immunization" process through the use of "systematic desensitization" but, though this effort failed, the therapeutic process continued to go on in the sessions.

The above formulation of the clinical issues that emerged from the behavioral analysis needs also to be contrasted with the concept of "homosexual panic" that would be employed in a psychoanalytic interpretation of the same events. Paul's efforts to get into a relationship with a woman and his ambivalence about this can be understood as indicating an "unconscious" conflict generated by his "latent homosexuality." Indeed, as will become evident in the description of the second major phase of treatment below, Paul was continually preoccupied with the fear of being homosexual. This fear, as events will subsequently show, had a special meaning for him that reflected the major issue of a fear of abandonment and entrapment rather than a specific concern about his sexual identification. When his fear of helplessness was reduced through various strategies and techniques, his fear of his "latent" homosexuality also was reduced and he was freed to contract an emotional relationship with a woman. He never got "insight" into his hypothetical "unconscious" homosexual strivings.

THE SECOND PHASE OF TREATMENT

The Eleventh Session

This session, in which treatment was resumed, occurred three weeks after Paul had terminated in February. He seemed quite tense this time on initial contact. The issue that brought him back was the fact that he had broken up his relationship with both Nan and Sue. He knew he precipitated the break with Nan. When she showed ambivalence again about breaking up with her boyfriend he had given her an ultimatum: it was to be either him or Paul. Nan chose to stay with her boyfriend. Paul panicked. He had gone too far. The dread began to come over him again as it had last summer. When Sue also got fed up with him because she said he was just using her for sex, his anxiety got even worse. Mostly, he felt isolated and alone, and had the fear that he would "lose control" and become insane. His anxiety was not consistently high; it ebbed by itself in the course of the day and then would rise again. He wasn't sure what reasons (that is, what events) set it off. One event, however, he was sure activated his anxiety. A woman he knew who lived nearby in a college dormitory committed suicide because she was rejected by her boyfriend. He worried that he, too, might commit suicide. This was the reason he called me.

There was another major issue that caused his anxiety to rise at this time.

He was beginning the second and final semester of his junior year. It was very important that he get good grades in order to be able to get into a good graduate school. This meant intensive studying and the heightened sense that he might not live up to the expectations of his father and his professors who thought so highly of him. Intensive study to stave off the peril of disapproval of authority persons also meant isolation from his friends and especially isolation from women. This isolation from women made him feel that he might end up a homosexual, go insane, and possibly commit suicide.

Paul had in this manner presented the issues that would occupy us for the remainder of his treatment over the following ten months.

I listened supportively during this session and restated the position that his anxiety was learned and needed to be unlearned. I explained the rationale undergirding Benson's Relaxation Response and taught him how to do it in the office. I contracted with him to do it twice a day at home until the following week.

A brief overview of what typically went on in the sessions that followed will be provided before addressing the major issues that were dealt with and the strategies employed in confronting them.

Paul came to each session ready to discuss the happenings of the previous week. He related these events and I characteristically responded by interpreting them in behavioral terms. Interpretation here meant looking with him at what had happened and giving meaning to these events in learning theory terms. Paul quickly got the idea and he assumed this same posture in understanding events as they occurred during the week. He "ordered the data," as he phrased it, and gave it meaning; thereby he reduced his confusion and the concomitant anxiety. He took notes between sessions on his monitoring of his own behavior. This clarification process was not understood, however, to be the goal of treatment—in a real sense it was the beginning. And there was not just one beginning. There were many beginnings. Having clarified an issue, we would undertake through the employment of a particular technique the modification of that behavior in feeling, thinking, or acting. Then we characteristically moved on to clarifying another issue. I introduced the various techniques I employed with him in the context of this process: "Let us see whether 'flooding' will work in reducing your paranoid feelings." "Perhaps we can interrupt your obsessive ruminations by 'thought stopping' or a combination of 'flooding' and 'thought stopping.' " Alternative ways of cognitively structuring what was going on through examining irrational assumptions based on previous learning were suggested when it was judged to be appropriate. I encouraged him to "move out" in confronting his father, in getting closer to a woman emotionally, in getting an apartment of his own, and in finding a summer job.

With each lifestyle change his anxiety lessened and his insights into his past and what was happening to him in the present broadened. The word "broadened" is here used purposively instead of the corollary "deepened." He indeed saw more clearly how his conflict originated in early experiences while growing up, but his major understanding of those current environmental events was that were maintaining his feelings of helplessness. He could see that the movement outward that began with the crisis of the previous summer progressively decreased his fears of abandonment and entrapment. It was really "broadsight" he had achieved more than "insight."

The Twelfth Session

He told me at the onset that Benson's Relaxation Response had only a mild effect. His anxiety still remained high. Furthermore, he was very self-conscious; just the previous night in the dining room he felt, in the midst of a crowd of fellow students, isolated and weird. He had been pondering about the origin of his anxiety. He noticed that the anxious mood seemed to "precede" the obsessive thinking that preoccupied him. He was becoming aware of "labeling" his mood states. It was after he felt the anxiety and dread that he thought he must be homosexual. This is what he had done the previous summer. His anxiety was thereby potentiated by this labeling process.

I reinforced his analysis of what was happening. I pointed out that it was the condition of "separation" that activated the chain of events he had described to me. Currently it was separation from the two girls in his life and also separation from his friends necessitated by the intensive studying he was doing. Last summer it was separation from his family and friends that seems to have activated his panic.

My interpretation seemed to be reducing his anxiety. I asked him halfway through the session to tell me how much anxiety he was experiencing. He said when he came in his anxiety was around 70 s.u.d.s (subjective units of disturbance)—it had dropped significantly. He was now only mildly anxious, around 20 s.u.d.s. He said it was because he felt relief in the realization that his anxiety was caused by specific events and that, therefore, he might be able to exert some control over it. He also pointed out that the intensity of his anxiety decreased when he was in the company of his friends (he was referring to his male friends); he was "strengthened" by talking to them. Paul was confirming my interpretation that the isolation he experienced when he closeted himself in his room to study intensified his anxiety. He was broadening his understanding of the interactive relationship between environmental events and intense psychological states.

The Next Four Sessions

In the following four sessions, Paul elaborated a major theme that until this point he had only dimly alluded to. He had done some thinking, he said, and had come to some conclusions. It was surprising to him that the reasons for his panic last summer had just become clear to him, now, in a period when he felt quite tense.

The origins of his separation anxiety, he could now see, occurred when his brother was born, when he was five years old. He was no longer the center of attention in his house. It was a very traumatic time. He remembers his mother withdrawing from him. He started bed wetting. Obviously, he said, it must have been to get his mother's attention. Paul then shifted immediately to talking about his having nocturnal emissions at the age of sixteen. He apprehensively confided to me that he was quite unable to masturbate during his adolescence and nocturnal emissions were the only source of relief of sexual tension. His nocturnal emissions, however, were a source of great embarrassment because they exposed that he had sexual feelings. He remembers worrying that his mother would find out and that this would result in losing her affection. "How about that for an Oedipal conflict?" He laughed as he tauntingly said this. I was sure he was challenging what he knew to be my behaviorist theoretical commitment. I responded by saying that this experience could also explain his sensitivity to rejection by authority figures and fear of disappointing his father's expectations of his academic performance. He felt reassured by my acceptance of his "Oedipal" interpretation.

He went on to elaborate further additional connections that he had made in understanding his current anxiety. The last summer, when he had been working and sleeping at the mental hospital and separated from his family and friends, he worried a great deal that he might have nocturnal emissions. This preoccupation resulted in his not being able to sleep for several nights. This stressful period immediately preceded the panic he experienced when the young man was admitted to the hospital in a floridly psychotic condition. Worn out by his lack of sleep and already having thought of "losing control" and going crazy, Paul felt quite vulnerable when the police informed the psychiatrist that the young man who was admitted was also a known "homosexual." What was previously a fear of being rejected because of sexual feelings now became intensified in the form of dread of total abandonment by friends and family because he might be found out to be a "faggot."

It should be noted at this point that Paul had never reported having homosexual feelings before this incident, nor did he experience any during the period that I saw him in treatment. I explored this at length with him. It was the fear of being labeled as a homosexual that panicked him, not such propensities. He was equally fearful of "going crazy," another form of losing control. Both of these preoccupations were manifestations of the more basic fear of abandonment that were triggered by the events that were described. In order to make a case for "latent" homosexuality in Paul one needs to posit the assumption that "unconscious," unresolved "pre-Oedipal conflicts" were at work.

Paul's obsessive need to have a sexual relationship with a woman was fueled by the need to allay his homosexual fears. Sex with Sue, devoid of emotional commitment, was surprisingly not effective in reassuring him. In fact, it left him depleted and depressed. It was, he said, too much like a nocturnal emission because there was no affection from Sue or himself associated with the sex. On the other hand, he could now see that when he had emotionally warm feelings toward a girl and experienced tender feelings from her, as he did from Nan, he was repelled by the experience—that also made him feel uncomfortable. The origins of Paul's ambivalence was becoming clearer to him. This clarification process, this "ordering of the events" in a manner that made sense to him (that is, in his terms, his "Oedipal conflict") appreciably reduced his anxiety. It did not resolve it, however. This insight was a necessary but not sufficient condition for change.

It seemed to me that, from a behavioral perspective, the next objective in the treatment process emanating from my enhanced clarification of issues that Paul had just experienced was to help him manage his anxiety about "loss of control." Consider that it is not the "content" of Paul's preoccupations that is to become the next focus in the treatment plan, but rather the anxiety as such which is activated by the fear of loss of control. His specific preoccupations with being homosexual, of going crazy, and of committing suicide are conceptualized as the manifest cognitive content of the basic fear of abandonment and of entrapment. The task from this theoretical perspective, then, becomes that of designing any appropriate technique that can make it possible for him to reduce this basic fear by gaining control over his nocturnal emissions. It would logically follow that if this could be accomplished his preoccupations about homosexuality and insanity would also be reduced. It could also be expected that getting closer to a woman emotionally would become easier because of the reduction of the fear of engulfment. His anxiety about getting close, acquired in his relationship with his mother, could also be expected to be reduced with an enhanced sense of control of his sexual feelings. His ambivalent strivings in relation to women would by definition, then, also be expected to be reduced in intensity.

The following technique was designed with Paul. The next time he had sex with Sue he was to withdraw when he felt close to ejaculation and to masturbate himself to the point of orgasm. He was, of course, to explain this procedure beforehand to Sue and to get her cooperation. Paul thought this was kind of weird but he would go along with it at least on an experimental basis. He was especially motivated because his difficulty in falling asleep lately due to the fear of having a nocturnal emission was getting worse. This difficulty, in turn, made him tired during the day and interrupted his studying which further exacerbated his anxiety. Since his tiredness during the day decreased his efficiency in mastering the material he was studying, he needed to spend more time alone in the library; this resulted in increased isolation from his friends, which further potentiated his anxiety.

The next session Paul arrived quite visibly pleased and he appeared more relaxed than I could recall ever seeing him before. "It worked," he announced dramatically. "I have been able to masturbate for the first time in my life." Paul reported sleeping well and feeling relaxed as a consequence throughout the day. His studying efficiency increased and he was able to spend more time socializing. The negative feedback system described above had been interrupted by his ability to reduce his sexual tension by masturbation. His fear of losing control was effectively "worked through" by the actual experience of being able to control the discharge of sexual tension. The fact that Paul was now capable of masturbating had "symbolic" meaning for him. It did not remain the preferred manner of achieving the reduction of sexual tension. While he, in fact, masturbated on occasion when he was alone—often before going to sleep—he continued his sexual relationship with Sue, which now was more satisfying.

The theoretical implications of this therapeutic outcome need to be elaborated a bit further. The insight into his conflict (the clarification process described above) resulted in some reduction of anxiety because his "understanding" of what was happening provided him with some modicum of control over his sense of helplessness. In a sense, he achieved some cognitive control in this manner. It was only when he was able to "do" something, however, at the conative level, if you will, that he was able to experience a sense of mastery over his anxiety. The "psychodynamics" of the conflict were resolved *without* his "working through" the issues in the traditional verbal fashion. The resolution of the conflict, furthermore, was a lasting one as subsequent events will show.

In fact, in the session after the one described above, Paul already began to talk about the changing character of his relationship to Sue. He experienced a feeling of caring for her that was absent before. In the weeks that followed this feeling deepened, and he was able to enter into an exclusive relationship with her. They were together all the time. The course of this relationship over the next eight months during which I saw Paul went through various phases. At times, his feelings of being engulfed by Sue returned and he experienced strong feelings of wanting to take distance from her. He felt at one period that having been, for the first time, successful in being emotionally close to a woman, he ought to be able to try it with another woman as well. And often times he had paranoid feelings when Sue seemed to show interest in a close friend of his. His worry about being homosexual reoccurred at one point when he was talking with a bisexual male student.

Paul, however, remained with Sue throughout these different phases. They moved together into an apartment during the following summer. They visited his parents in his home town for an extended vacation at the end of the summer; he remained basically contented during the fall and until the time I terminated with him the following December. His weekly descriptions of the evolution of this relationship with Sue left no doubt that it had become a mutually nurturing and strengthening one.

The reduction of his fear of "losing control" through the approach described above constituted a major breakthrough in Paul's treatment. A great deal of work was left to be done, but he had been "stabilized," so to speak. His overall anxiety had lessened. He no longer felt compelled to use the sessions primarily to unburden himself of the worries of the week and was not limited to getting relief through cognitive control (i.e., understanding) and through the "support" he got from me in the context of our therapeutic alliance. He was now able to "step back" and to utilize the various techniques that I made available to him for coping with the various sources of anxiety that he experienced.

The Next Five Sessions

It was in the next five sessions (April 8 to May 20) that a great deal of the more classical behavioral work was accomplished. Consider that Paul was gearing up for the final exams of his junior year. This was a critical period since his final grades this semester would determine, at least in his mind, his chances of being accepted into a "good" graduate school. The pressure to excel was intensified and so was his obsessive ruminative behavior. He was alert to any sign or cue in the environment that he might fail, not only academically but in every other way as a person. When Sue went away for any length of time—in terms of hours, not days—he was sure she had abandoned him. When she was with him for a sustained period of time, he felt engulfed by her. This "negative scanning" was especially evident in the classroom where at times it seemed to reach paranoid proportions. His professor seemed sullen when he looked at him. He was sure he had lost confidence in him and would fail him in one course and refuse to write a letter of recommendation for him. He compared himself to other students constantly and found himself wanting. His ambivalence about making the most mundane kinds of choices (where to eat dinner) was exacerbated. He had to take the Graduate Record Exam and he knew he would do badly. He worried that he would get into an accident, that he would develop homosexual feelings toward a man, and about other things.

The intensity of these catastrophizing preoccupations varied widely throughout the week. A variety of techniques were employed to bring them under control.

He agreed finally to do Benson's Relaxation Response twice a day, before breakfast and before dinner. This was designed as a background measure to raise his anxiety threshold. It also made it possible for him to experience some control since he could do something that had an immediate effect on reducing his discomfort.

I instructed him to monitor more carefully his catastrophizing thoughts.

This now involved recording, in writing, what time the thoughts occurred and what he was doing and feeling at the time. It was very important to identify the actual triggering event, such as the professor's sullen look, the awareness of Sue's absence, and so forth. In the session we now, together, extracted the major theme that characterized the various ruminative thoughts he was describing and that led to a sense of helplessness and powerlessness.

The careful daily monitoring of those life events that were causally related to the intensification of his anxiety resulted in a diminution of his distress. The "control" that this monitoring process afforded was due to the additional distancing and objectification of the environment stimuli or causes of his anxiety that it provided. He now experienced his anxiety in a different kind of existential sense as a process with identifiable properties such as intensity, duration, and with a beginning and an end. His self-criticism and scrupulosity were relieved by the freedom he was able to gain from his previous characterological understanding of what was happening to him. He no longer worried about himself having "deep-seated" unconscious conflicts over which he had no control. His fear of going "crazy" and his fear of his latent homosexuality, as he himself labeled it, were markedly decreased as a consequence of focusing on his interaction with the environment, rather than on his intrapsychic processes. The other techniques employed potentiated this therapeutic effect.

The next procedure for the treatment of obsessive-ruminative behavior that I taught him is described by Rachman (Rachman, Hodgson, & Marks, 1971). I instructed Paul to set aside two 45-minute periods in which he would practice this "flooding" technique. I described the details of the implementation of this technique in the interview room and had him practice it in my presence.

First, he was instructed to achieve a deep level of relaxation by the Benson Method. This took him only about three or four minutes, since by now he had some experience with this method. Next, he was to allow himself to ruminate freely, with his eyes closed, about whatever in the normal course of the day triggered his anxious thoughts. He was to actively scan and search out images, situations of the previous day or week that made him anxious, and to recreate the anxious mood that accompanied them. In the training session in my office I fed him stimuli, i.e., images, from situations he had related to me in previous sessions. I monitored the amount of anxiety that they aroused by asking him to rate on a scale of 0–100 how much anxiety he was experiencing at a particular point in time. (Rachman's studies have shown that long exposure times at low levels of intensity result in more efficacious reduction of anxiety in individuals who ruminate obsessively.) I controlled the intensity of his anxiety to a level below 30 s.u.d.s. I did this by testing the anxiety evoking potential of different images (his professor looking at him in a sullen way versus Sue's being away for a long period of time), and I also varied the duration of his exposure to a particular image. He was instructed to let it go if his anxiety exceeded 40 s.u.d.s. He could later come back to it. During a 45-minute session, then, several different situations could be focused on for varying periods of time and with varying, but controlled, degrees of intensity. What happens from a learning theory perspective is that an extinction process takes place. The stimulus response connections between the anxiety-evoking images and the anxiety response is weakened through a "saturation" effect. Also, the effect is expected to generalize to *in vivo* (real life) situations. In Paul's case this is indeed what happened. Over the next five weeks, practicing this procedure twice a day at home, he reported he experienced a marked reduction in anxiety that he attributed to the "flooding" he was doing.

There is another aspect to this procedure that needs to be described. Paul was also instructed to "thought stop" at those times during the day, other than his flooding practice sessions, when obsessive thoughts would occur spontaneously. We practiced "thought stopping" in the office. He was instructed to conjure up a negative thought and the second he felt the accompanying anxiety to shout "stop" to himself subvocally in order to interrupt, to "short circuit," the stimulus-response sequence. He was cautioned that when thought stopping is first tried by an individual there is often an increase rather than a decrease in the rate at which obsessive ruminative thoughts will occur. Continued perserverance, however, would result in a subsequent period when the incidence would decrease.

I had also included "cognitive restructuring" among the techniques that might help Paul to manage his anxiety. I had in fact instructed him in the Meichenbaum (1977) version that involves identifying a negative thought as a discriminative one in order to activate a sequence of events, which included relaxing by the Benson Method and the "turning on" corrective self-statements —that is, more reality oriented thoughts that could interrupt the catastrophizing effect of previously learned thoughts and feelings. This method was only mildly effective with Paul. The pressure of his negative thoughts (i.e., "I will fail in my exams, Sue will abandon me, I won't be able ever to make a decent living if I fail academically") was often so strong that they overrode his cognitive restructuring efforts, and left him feeling even more helpless and powerless. The "flooding" technique described above was more suited to him at this time.

It was my helping him to structure his week, however, that proved to be the most effective strategy in reducing his anxiety. We reviewed together his daily activities on an hourly basis and Paul, it became evident, tended to attempt to study for long periods without breaks. His productivity would decrease over time which raised his anxiety and caused an intensification of his study effort; this, in turn, left no time for socializing and resulted in his feeling isolated, deprived, and angry. Sue's support mitigated his anxiety, but often after a period of time (usually after long periods of uninterrupted study) he would begin to experience her presence as engulfing. We interrupted these patterns by planning together his week on an hourly basis, which provided a more reasonable balance between work and play. He understood the nonproductive character of his frenzied study habits and his "guilt" when not studying was further controlled by the fact that I had "prescribed" pleasurable activities as an antidote to nonproductive studying.

Paul's anxiety was markedly reduced by this structuring effort. He "contracted" with me to take specified periods off for recreation and each week reported on his subjective experiences in following this new regimen. I provided the "support" he needed in overcoming the ambivalence and discomfort that was generated by his taking "time off." It was the increased efficiency in mastering his course work, however, that in the end consolidated his adherence to this more appropriate regimen.

Paul took his final exams and did well.

THE FINAL PHASE OF TREATMENT

The final period of treatment encompassed the three summer months and extended to the beginning of December when treatment was terminated. I saw Paul during this time for 21 more sessions.

This period was characterized by important "lifestyle changes," or individuation experiences. It had become evident to me and to Paul over the last few months of treatment that Paul's anxiety was generated because he was reaching that point in his life requiring, rather demanding, that he individuate. His psychological "maturation" had been truncated in a home environment that did not allow for graduated periods of separation, and from a family where mutual interdependence and enmeshment were the established modes of relating. Paul, at college, had transported his family structure to the campus by his close association with Hillel house, by limiting his social contacts to other Jewish students. Paul felt engulfed by his parents and sibling, and yet had a very low threshold for feelings of abandonment and loss. This was the conflict that came to a head the summer he worked at the mental hospital and that preceded his returning to college for his junior year. This experience was the proximate precipitating event that activated his panic. Other events in his daily experiences also stimulated his anxiety reactions, such as developing a close relationship to Sue, finishing college, and so forth. These events were functionally related to the onset and maintenance of his anxiety reactions. These events, however, constituted a series of steps he was taking to separate himself from his family. The specific techniques employed to manage his anxiety in these different situations, then, need to be understood in the broader context of facilitating basic behavioral or lifestyle changes that are labeled "individuation." Paul was "extinguishing" the feelings of anxiety that had been maintained in a negatively reinforcing manner by continued attachments to his mother, his father, and his brother. It was now time for him to "move out"; that is, to rearrange the conditions of his life in a manner that would further facilitate and consolidate his independence. Paul needed to experience the fact that he could exist, survive emotionally, and thrive without the continued dependence on his family and family surrogates. This was not to say that Paul would not need their "support" in the sense of knowing they cared for him and that he could rely on them. It did mean that he would need to sever the "symbiotic" bond to them that left him feeling helpless and powerless at the slightest cue that he was being rejected by them or by anyone else who was important to him. The work of this last phase of treatment was centered on helping Paul make these "structural" changes.

After final exams, Paul rented an apartment in Boston; this was the first time in his life he had ever lived alone. He had suggested doing this and I strongly supported him. It was a very difficult two weeks of adjustment. Sue had gone home for a month's vacation. Paul felt like he was "going to die," so intense was his anxiety at being alone. I saw him twice that week. I merely listened, gave him "support." Paul managed OK—a kind of *in vivo* (real life) flooding took place. Within two days after he moved in his anxiety "peaked," got very intense, and then began to subside gradually over the rest of this two-week period. We had predicted this together in the therapeutic sessions. He knew what was coming and was cognitively prepared for it. He also maintained contact with his male friends and called Sue frequently, in addition to seeing me. He did Benson's regularly twice a day. Paul, then, was not without "support" during this transitional period, but this "support" was the kind that reinforced his strengths and validated his capacity to cope, rather than the kind that provided an escape from the situation.

Paul had taken this apartment because of a summer job he had been able to get through his department to do sociological type research in a ghetto area of Boston. This constituted another important step in "moving out." His job required him to associate with low income people living in housing projects. It was, from a therapeutic perspective, an ideal kind of activity for Paul to be engaged in. Daily he was required to interview strangers in their homes. He had never before met people who were so different from him. He was anxious at first, but his anxiety diminished rapidly after only a few interviews. He also did a good job and was reinforced for this by his professor. He got into it and actually began to enjoy what he was doing.

A month after he had taken this apartment Sue returned and moved in with him. He felt as though he was married. It was good most of the time but, at times, his feelings of being engulfed by her returned. These periods were short lived, however. He took Sue home with him to meet his parents. They liked her. They didn't "go crazy" as he sort of expected. They visited Sue's parents. Her father didn't like Paul. It didn't bother him much.

A close friend of Paul's came to Boston during the latter part of the summer and stayed in his apartment. One morning, while Paul was on the train going to work, he began to feel that his friend was "making it" with Sue in his absence. He had distance from these feelings, however. He knew they were "paranoid." He talked to Sue about them. She laughed and reassured him. The feelings reoccurred again while his friend was still there, but with less intensity. He used "thought stopping" to control them. It worked some of the time.

Then at other times Paul wanted to experiment with other women. These urges, however, lacked the urgency they had had previously. Gradually, they dropped out and occurred only infrequently.

In September Paul began his senior year. He was very anxious about the Graduate Record Exam he had to take and ambivalent about the career he wanted to pursue. His father encouraged him to forget about sociology and pursue a more traditional career like medicine or law. Paul and I reviewed this issue and sorted out his own proclivities from those of his father. He managed his anxiety well in taking the Graduate Record Exam. He continued to live with Sue and their relationship deepened. He felt "good," he felt "strong." He was anxiety free most of the time. There were relapses, old fears came back from time to time, but he managed them well and they were of short duration. Paul decided what career he wanted to pursue. His final course exams in December were uneventful. Paul was clearly on a different track. We had set a termination date, the beginning of November or December, just before the winter recess.

7

A Case History of a Person with
a Contamination Phobia

Millie Collingsworth's presenting problem was a contamination phobia which she had been suffering from since puberty, around the time of the onset of menstruation. A complex set of decontamination rituals had developed over the years that extended far beyond the original need to clean herself after her period and permeated her entire lifestyle. Her daily life was structured around the need to wash at frequent intervals after she touched and thereby contaminated different things she came into contact with, including her own body. Her choice of spouse, her sexual habits, her choice of friends, the kind of occupation she chose, and her abuse of alcohol constituted a complex system of behaviors that, together with the symptom, maintained her avoidance of sexual feelings which had become associated with the experience of intense anxiety. The treatment strategy that was designed took this complexity into account. The elimination of the symptom, in this case undertaken first, constituted only one of the foci in this "field" of interrelated events (Spiegel, 1971).

Millie Collingsworth was referred to me by a psychiatrist who had seen her for about six sessions and who decided with her that behavior therapy was the preferred modality for the problem she had presented. This was the "compulsion" to engage in decontamination rituals throughout the day which were progressively encroaching on ever larger parts of her life. Furthermore, she did not impress him during this brief number of sessions as being open to insight through the traditional psychodynamic mode of treatment.

I inquired as to how he felt when he continued to see her while I dealt with the compulsive symptom. He was worried about the effects on her of removing her symptom and intimated vaguely that this could precipitate a psychotic

episode. I told him that I sometimes made this arrangement with some therapists, although in most cases it did not work out because the predictable could
be counted on to happen. The patient would use the psychodynamic therapist
to avoid the anxiety-evoking conditions that he/she would be working on in
behavior therapy. We agreed this issue would be resolved after I saw his patient for the initial evaluation.

When I talked to the patient on the phone to arrange the initial interview, I
heard a woman who was obviously ambivalent about seeing me and whose
"resistance," as I had already begun to formulate it in my mind, took the
form of an inability to comprehend the instructions on how to get to my office. Her tone of voice reflected an impatience with my ineptness in describing the best route and her southern accent was quite pronounced. "The vibes
are not right," I thought to myself. "This may never get off the ground. It
sounds like she's not ready and that she is accommodating her psychiatrist."
She later told me that after this phone call, she almost decided to cancel the
appointment because she was sure she was not going to like me. I sounded,
among other things, much younger than I actually turned out to be.

THE INITIAL INTERVIEW

The initial interview did not go in the direction I had expected it would on the
basis of the telephone conversation. She related easily, was articulate (her
southern accent seemed to be less pronounced), and impressed me as motivated with a considerable degree of sophisticated psychological understanding.
(I speculated that this was an outcome of the therapy she had with the referring psychiatrist.)

I began the behavioral analysis by exploring the history of the problem for
which she had been referred—the compulsive symptom. She responded to my
initial inquiry by inquiries of her own. How much experience had I with this
kind of problem? How long did I think it would take? Had I talked to her psychiatrist, Dr. Hersh, and what had we talked about?

I responded to each of these questions directly. In the process of doing so, I
had begun the reculturization process. In regard to my experience with this
kind of problem, I shared with her my understanding that most behavior disorders were "learned" and specific procedures were employed by behavior
therapists for their "unlearning." I had treated several patients with contamination phobias successfully, but this did not mean that I could guarantee her
success.

Mrs. Collingsworth is of medium height, her body build is slight, her facial
features chiseled in a classic form, her hair, a sandy brown color, is carefully
coiffured. Her clothing, in contrast to the care she obviously gave to makeup,

grooming, and so forth, was casual, not particularly well-fitted, and more in the campus style that is preferred by college women. She moved casually and spoke softly, yet she conveyed a feeling of controlled agitation.

I shared with her my confidence in the efficacy of the procedures employed with this kind of problem, but I concurrently conveyed the understanding that success was also contingent on the individual's readiness for change. People are ready for change at different times in their lives, I told her, and readiness was related to how uncomfortable their behavior problems had become. She said she was ready. She was afraid the problem was getting worse; she could see herself "going all the way"—that is, deciding that everything she touched was contaminated and she would become paralyzed by having to wash herself constantly. Furthermore, the fear of contamination had generalized to objects touched by others which she, therefore, felt compelled to avoid touching, such as the sink in the ladies room at work. She avoided going to the bathroom, for example, during the six-hour period she was at the office where she worked as an executive secretary for an advertising company.

I asked her to describe a typical day so that I might understand better what she was experiencing. I specifically asked that she detail as much as possible exactly what happened hourly throughout the day. I had decided at this point to postpone taking a detailed history of the symptom since it was very clear that the patient wanted to tell me about what was going on now, in her current life, and to share her hurt and her fear with me.

The rapport between us was good and I decided that by focusing on the present I could also make significant gains in consolidating the therapeutic alliance at this very early phase of treatment.

When she first gets out of bed she goes immediately to the bathroom and washes her hands, since they have become contaminated during the night because of her sexual activity with her husband and because she has touched the "lower part of her own body." She then goes into the shower, where she washes her body carefully "from top to bottom" with the exception of her face. While washing herself in the shower, she counts the number of times she soaps each area of her body and feels ready to go on to the next one only when she has done so twelve times. The number twelve has no special significance, she says. She wipes herself with her own towel and then goes to the sink and washes her hands again because she has touched her genitals in the shower, which are the most contaminated part of her body. She does not wipe her hands with a towel; instead she puts on a terry cloth bathrobe, shakes off the excess water from her hands and herself. She first dresses the upper part of her body (bra, blouse, etc.) and then her lower body (panties, dress or slacks) which involves touching her body and again requires her to wash her hands at the sink. She then washes her face, which was not touched while in the shower; finally she brushes her teeth which completes her cleansing functions. Why does she leave her face for last? She wants to be sure it is absolutely clean before she puts on her makeup. She is now completely decontaminated and, therefore, must take precautions that she not contaminate herself the rest of the day. These precautions involve not touching or not being touched by objects in her environment that are potentially contaminating; this includes her cat—she is especially careful about her cat's not rubbing against her legs when she goes downstairs in the morning. She is also very careful not to touch her legs or any part of her lower body throughout the day. If she does so, she must decontaminate by washing her hands. Her lower body, therefore, is both a source of contamination and, when decontaminated by showering, an area that must not be recontaminated by being touched by contaminated objects from the outside. (The sexual connotations here emerge in sharp relief.) She opens the door to the cellar with a kleenex. She picks up the morning newspaper with a kleenex. The front door knob is turned with a kleenex.

She does not go to the bathroom throughout the six hours she is at work. She is "automatically constipated" and she has trained her bladder to hold out until she gets out of work. When, on occasion, she does go to the bathroom at work, she arranges to do so during the lunch hour so that the half hour she needs to decontaminate herself will not be noticed. Decontamination involves washing her hands repeatedly until she is satisfied they are decontaminated, and then using kleenex to open the door to come out. Often she inadvertently touches the doorknob or the sink just when she has finished washing herself, and so she must begin the process all over again.

When the "red tide" comes once a month things are especially difficult. Her sense of being unclean is more intense and the time spent in the shower, bathroom, etc., is much longer. Also, she cannot wear slacks while having her period; she feels more vulnerable because more of her clothing is directly touching her body and, therefore, more susceptible to contamination.

When she leaves work at three o'clock, she typically goes out for a drink with two of her friends who work for the same firm. She has at least two drinks, often three at this time. She then goes food shopping or to the local mall to browse in the stores, and arrives home at about 5:30 when her husband is also scheduled to arrive from work. They have another cocktail or two before dinner, wine or beer during dinner, and sometimes a drink after dinner.

She avoids housework as much as she can because of her problem. Her husband doesn't mind that their house is not clean most of the time. Evenings typically are spent reading or watching television. Her husband watches a lot of television. She describes her husband, a computer analyst for a large Boston firm, as an "easygoing" person, "very lovable," but also quite passive. He is very tolerant of her problem.

THE NEXT FIVE SESSIONS

The next two sessions were devoted to expanding the behavioral analysis both vertically and horizontally in the manner described in Chapter 2. I inquired both into the history of the symptom itself and broadened my understanding of the social context in which the patient currently functioned. I concurrently began to formulate a treatment plan and shared the reasoning that went into this formulation with the patient. I decided early that the presenting symptom needed to be addressed first because of its debilitating effect on the patient's life, and also because of her very high motivation for change that emerged in the initial session. I felt I had to capitalize on this. Also the patient impressed me in this initial session as being at a place where she had stable support structures: principally a rewarding job, close friends, and a satisfying marital relationship that could serve to reduce to tolerable dimensions the anxiety incumbent in giving up the symptom. These support persons could serve the function, in other words, of mitigating the anxiety incumbent in giving up the rituals. I shared these impressions with the referring psychiatrist. He agreed to a moratorium on his treatment until I had completed the behavior therapy with her. She agreed to this.

Mrs. Collingsworth informed me in the second session that she was born and grew up in the south. Her parents were strict Baptists with very clear notions about morality, which were fortified Sunday at church services that the patient always attended. The notion of hell and damnation for sexual transgressions was mediated early. Her early home environment, however, was in other respects a warm and loving one. She felt close to both her mother and her father, and she recalls no traumatic events during her childhood; the one large exception is her experiences around menstruation. She was not well-prepared. She recalls her mother talking to her about it in vague terms she had not fully comprehended. When she finally did menstruate, she recalls feeling unclean and there was a distinct psychological sense of sinfulness that accompanied the physical sensation of bleeding. Her mother gave her a sanitary napkin; she remembers it impressed her as being unclean once it was put on her, so she washed her hands after using it. Then the panties she wore when she menstruated were felt to be unclean and so not to be touched. Then the faucet she touched when she washed her hands after handling her kotex or her panties. And then the clothes she wore over her panties were contaminated and so she had to wash after dressing. Her daily shower now took on much greater importance in her life, since it gradually began to serve the purpose of decontaminating. Now the sink itself became contaminated, not just the faucet, and the doorknobs in her house, since they had been touched by people who had touched the sink that she had touched and thereby contaminated. She stopped cleaning her room because it was contaminated by her having walked into it.

During the third interview, I expanded the history-taking to get a sense of the background of the patient. I tried to cover social and cultural areas, as well as psychological areas. I did a lot of reculturization in this session; that is, I reacted first in more detail to the information she had given me the previous session. I elaborated the theme that her early learned associations of sin to sexual feelings were activated during puberty and were localized in the menstruation experience itself. It was a predictably traumatic event for her since it was an uncontrollable development that left her feeling helpless and vulnerable to the sexual feelings that are emergent in that period of a woman's life. Cleaning reduced that fear. The initial focus of her uncleanness, her genital area, generalized to include that broad range of objects and situations she had described. The cleaning rituals served to reduce her anxiety. They, too, are learned responses and can be unlearned. So can the anxiety response to the situations that activate it.

I responded to her questions and clarified issues related to this theme and then continued the behavioral analysis. I did one other thing in this session; I introduced her to Benson's Relaxation Response. I taught her how to do it and briefly elaborated the rationale for its employment as part of a total treatment strategy that I would review with her later. I did this at the end of the session. She was skeptical about its value and didn't think she'd like doing it, but she agreed to try it.

Mrs. Collingsworth told me that her early childhood, as she recalls it, was generally uneventful. She grew up in the deep South during the fifties and was not exposed to the social strains that characterized efforts of the Blacks to achieve integration during that period.She went to an upper-middle-class school in a comfortable suburb of one of the larger southern cities. Her father was a lawyer; her mother had gone to a two-year finishing woman's college. She was the oldest child and has a sister who is three years younger and a brother five years her junior. They still live in the south; both went to southern colleges. Her sister is married; her brother is not.

She, in contrast to her siblings, wanted to go to a northern school. No, it was not to get away from anything; she just felt more adventurous than her sister and brother. Her parents agreed, on the condition that she pick a school in the Boston area where her mother's sister lived. She agreed. She went to a four-year college, lived at the dormitory and visited with her aunt and her aunt's husband on weekends. Her aunt did not know about her problem during this period. In fact, she was able to perform her decontamination rituals in a manner that did not interfere with her school work or with her social relationships.

She had many good girlfriends, and associated in particular with three of them much of the time. She socialized a lot more in college than she had in high school. In retrospect, she realized what a spoiled person she was. She matured a great deal during those four years. She wondered how her good friends tolerated her self-centered behavior. She also found that she was very sensitive to being criticized and was gradually able to overcome this.

She started dating men in her freshman year in college. She had no problem with sexual overtures since there was no conflict; that is, it was out of the question, and she made this clear at the onset. Besides, while two of her friends had sex regularly, the third one didn't, and so she did not feel all that different. It helped when she met her future husband, Ralph, at the end of her freshman year and dated him almost exclusively for the remainder of her college career. He was also inhibited sexually, and while they necked a lot he responded readily to the limits that she set.

When Millie graduated college with a major in fine arts, she became engaged to Ralph, whom she was not to marry for another five years. Why? Well, neither of them felt ready. In fact, she was the one who in the end pushed for setting a marriage date. Ralph promptly broke off the engagement. He dated other women and she other men for about a year, but then they got together again.

During this estrangement period Millie became very upset and sought the help of a psychiatrist whom she saw on a once-a-week basis for a year. He didn't help her much, she said. Her contamination phobia was discussed; he probed for early childhood experiences and focused on her relationship to her parents. The therapy didn't go anywhere but it did, she said, give her the support she needed to hold herself together and also to initiate a reconciliation with Ralph. After this reconciliation, which occurred about a year before they got married, they began having full sexual intercourse. She does not recall being particularly disturbed the first time. Ralph had had some experience by then, and he was gentle with her. They do not have a sexual problem now, she said. They have sex about twice a month. Frequency is determined in part by their having agreed to have sex only during the "safe" period of the month. He wears a condom. She will not take the pill and never considered an I.U.D. She doesn't want children; a baby would be contaminated during birth. Ralph doesn't want children, either. She told me that she calls the shots at home. She yells a lot at Ralph. He is such a nice guy, who will do anything she asks.

Mrs. Collingsworth had no specific career plans when she graduated college, nor was there any specific kind of work she was particularly interested in doing. She had vague ideas of working in a large corporation in order to be around a lot of people. She started out by working in an industrial firm outside of Boston as a secretary. She had acquired skills in typing and shorthand, along the way; actually, her mother had insisted she take courses in these skills during the summer between academic years that she spent at home "because she might need them some day." Her first job lasted three months. She was a lousy typist and her shorthand skills were even less developed. She took, and lost, two more jobs in rapid succession; each job averaged around six months. In the meantime, her secretarial skills were getting better; at the time she saw me she had been working for over three years in an advertising agency. The job was not extremely demanding; furthermore, she was able to start work at nine and leave at three in the afternoon. This was important since she was able to, for the most part, get through this short day without going to the bathroom.

She had been married to Ralph for a year and a half when she came to see me. She was not able to identify any precipitating events related to the worsening of the compulsive symptoms that had taken her to see Dr. Hersh. No, there were no major changes in her life or traumatic events. She showed impatience in my dogged pursuance of a causal link to the exacerbation of her contamination phobia. Their plan not to have children had not changed. Where had I gotten the idea that this could be an issue? Ralph's work was coming along fine. His firm was growing and he was enjoying his job as a computer analyst. No, she didn't miss her parents. She called home once a week and that was all. Her father was getting ready to retire. They saw Ralph's parents on the average of once a month; no, there were no strains there, either. She couldn't stand her mother-in-law, but then she didn't need to like her because she saw her infrequently. During the summer they made a ritualistic trip south by car because she was afraid to fly, and stayed with her parents for about ten days. "Could we get on with it now?" she wondered aloud. She agreed to do Benson's Relaxation Response since I thought it was so important, but it sure sounded stupid to her.

Mrs. Collingsworth reported to me at the onset of the next session that her efforts to do the Benson's Relaxation Response did not go well. She couldn't concentrate for 20 minutes, it did not relax her, and furthermore she did not intend to try it again. It was a most frustrating experience for her.

I next attempted in this session to prepare the patient for systematic desensitization by initiating imagery training. My rationale, which I shared with her, was because she was not doing Benson's Relaxation Response, I wanted to try another technique to reduce the stress she would experience when we addressed the symptom directly through the "response prevention" procedure I would shortly describe to her. Systematic desensitization was a way of "rehearsing," so to speak, in imagination the procedure she would be undergoing for real. I then proceeded to tell her what the "response prevention" procedure was. We would order the situations in which she performed her decontamination rituals on a scale from most to least disturbing. I explained what I meant by this; I would ask her to assess subjectively how much anxiety she would experience if she did not perform a particular cleaning ritual. She was to assign a numerical value to each of these situations on a scale of 0–100, with 100 representing a "blind panic" level of anxiety and 0 representing no anxiety at all. Mrs. Collingsworth understood. I would next contract with her to enter a situation where she would feel contaminated; that is, to allow herself to be unclean in a particular situation and then to prevent herself from engaging in the decontamination ritual. I would start with situations low on the anxiety scale and gradually over several weeks build up to the most anxiety-provoking one. However, before I actually contracted with her to desist from performing the ritualistic cleansing behavior in a particular situation, we would desensitize her here in the office to that situation employing the systematic desensitization technique.

I next undertook, in this session, to do imagery training with her in preparation for "systematic desensitization." I next explored with her which low anxiety situation she might want to begin with so that I could illustrate for her the systematic desensitization technique. She chose touching her cat when coming downstairs in the morning. I instructed her to close her eyes and relax fully for a few minutes; then I asked her to imagine herself walking downstairs in the morning, touching her cat, and then proceeding to get her breakfast without washing her hands. She reported experiencing 50 degrees of anxiety when exposed to this scene. I exposed her to this scene repeatedly over the next 20 minutes, taking pains to be sure she was imagining fully and that she employed all sensory modalities to make the experience as close to her actually being in the situation as possible. Her anxiety had gone down to 30 s.u.d.s (subjective units of disturbance) at the end of 20 minutes.

Her "homework assignment" for the next session was to bring in the hierarchically ordered list of situations where she performed her decontamination phobias, and to practice the "touching her cat" scene once a day for 20 minutes.

In the fourth session a week later, Mrs. Collingsworth started off by telling me that the systematic desensitization also went badly. She just could not do it at home the way she was able to do it here in my office. She had trouble constructing realistic-feeling images. Furthermore, she didn't like it. The patient also mediated to me the clear meaning that she was not going to respond positively to my efforts to work with her on increasing her skill in constructing images. She liked the "idea" of systematic desensitization even less than Benson's Relaxation Response.

At this juncture I was faced with the question of whether or not to persevere in my efforts to induct the patient into these two techniques through a continued supportive stance. With some patients this low key supportive but firm approach works because it serves to reduce their anxiety about "letting go," "losing control," and so forth. With Mrs. Collingsworth I was convinced that this was going to be a futile effort. She was gearing up for a control struggle and I was not going to buy into it. Besides, we were still in the early alliance-building phase of the treatment and I did not intend to jeopardize my relationship with her. I chose to risk initiating a pattern of her shaping me out of following through with procedures that seemed appropriate at the time. I felt that a confrontation with her about control was inevitable, but that I had a chance of dealing with it once a therapeutic alliance had been formed.

The patient did bring to the session the list of situations in which she felt

contaminated and had ordered them on a scale of least to most anxiety-provoking. I felt this was an offering to me—a message from her that she was willing
to go halfway toward meeting any expectation that she be committed to a
therapeutic program.

I next explained to her the rationale undergirding the "response prevention" technique. I reviewed in a very nontechnical manner the results of the
clinical research using this method and made a strong case for its efficacy in
eliminating compulsive symptoms like hers. Pains were taken to make clear
that she could expect to experience high levels of anxiety when she prevented
herself from performing the decontaminating rituals and that this exposure
to anxiety constituted the therapeutic process itself. The anxiety would subside, or "extinguish," when she persevered in not performing the stress-
relieving, cleaning behavior. Our job was to design treatment strategy in which
she would be exposed to situations where she could not avoid the stress of
feeling contaminated by engaging in decontamination behaviors. This would
assure her the "extinction" process would occur sufficiently often for the
therapy to work. The "contracting" method was important in this regard
and I outlined how it was used. She thought that this "contracting" idea was
a good one. Her husband, she volunteered, could be recruited to help her
when the going got tough. He could help by giving her support to tolerate the
stress she knew she would experience when she desisted from performing her
cleaning rituals. "How did her husband feel about her contamination phobias?" I asked. "Well," she said, "it didn't bother him very much so he
didn't have much to say about it." The fact that their house wasn't cleaned
very often didn't bother him very much; when it really got bad he cleaned it
himself.

The question of the degree to which the patient's husband was maintaining
her symptoms emerged as an issue for me at this juncture, but I decided not to
explore it with the patient. I felt that the issue would be clarified when we instituted the "response prevention intervention program." Her husband's reaction to her increased freedom from the symptoms would be an index of his
investment in maintaining them. Other obvious issues in relation to her husband needed to also be explored at a later point. I was thinking primarily
about the effect of this symptom on their sex life; I wondered too about the
patient's excessive drinking and its meaning in relation to the symptom, in
particular, and to her marital relationship in general. The immediate task,
however, was to deal directly with the symptom.

Mrs. Collingsworth ordered the situations where she felt dirtied and so
compelled to decontaminate herself from least to most anxiety-evoking:

1. Touching the cat
2. Picking up the morning newspaper
3. Opening the cellar door

 4. Touching the doorknob of the main entrance door of the house
 5. Touching the television selector knob
 6. Touching the dishwasher handle
 7. Touching other assorted and unspecified objects in the kitchen "too numerous to mention right now"
 8. After completing shower and walking out of the shower stall
 9. After dressing upper half of her body—putting on brassiere and top
10. After dressing lower part of her body, i.e., stockings, panties, etc.
11. After brushing her teeth (the next to the last cleansing before she leaves the bathroom)
12. After the final morning hygiene act, brushing her teeth
13. Touching the bathroom doorknob as she leaves the bathroom
14. Just before she gets into bed with her husband to have sex
15. After she has sex with her husband and has thereby touched the lower part of his body
16. Touching her own body below the waist after she had decontaminated herself in the morning
17. Changing her kotex during menstruation
18. The most anxiety-provoking situation is touching the faucet in the bathroom or in the kitchen "because this is how it started"; meaning that the fear of dirtying the faucets after touching herself when she changed her kotex is the first instance she can remember of her fear of dirtiness spreading to objects outside of her own body.

This list, she cautioned me, was not exhaustive, but she felt it was generally representative and it would provide sufficient concrete behaviors for us to get started. I agreed.

I contracted with her to touch the cat and desist from washing her hands afterward as the initial "response prevention trial." She would do this once each day over the next seven days and we would review this experience the following session.

In the fifth session, the patient reported that it was surprisingly easy for her to prevent herself from washing her hands in the morning when she touched the cat. The first time she did it she had a small amount of apprehension, but this dissipated over the next few days. She could see, however, that it would not be as easy with other behaviors on her list; therefore, she started doing Benson's Relaxation Response and it was going well. I did not reinforce her at this point by saying "great" for the obvious reason that it could be interpreted as gratification on my part at her "capitulation" to my original suggestion. She said she wanted to move up the list, but not necessarily in the hierarchical order she had positioned the different items. She wanted to next start on the bathroom rituals because she felt these were more difficult and yet more relevant. I asked her which ones she wanted to contract for; she said she would put on her bra and blouse and not wash before she proceeded to dress the lower part of her body. In other words, she would dress completely without stopping to wash her hands.

I was very supportive of her in this session, mostly through nonverbal ways, like nodding, among others. I felt that the therapeutic alliance was developing. I cautioned her not to attempt too much too soon. She wanted more assurance that her anticipated anxiety would eventually decrease after she desisted from performing the decontamination rituals. She asked more questions about Benson's Relaxation Response. I explained that the contracts were cumulative; that is, each week the newly contracted behaviors would be added on to those contracted for the week before, until we had covered all of them. The pace of adding new ones each week would be regulated by both of us. My task was to help her deal with problems that might arise along the way. Her job was to share with me her thoughts and feelings as they arose along the way; the success of our venture was contingent to a large extent on open and frank communication between us.

THE NEXT EIGHT SESSIONS

These sessions were characterized by progressive movement through the items on Mrs. Collingsworth's list. She continued with the bathroom situation and contracted next to wash herself completely in the shower, and not leave her face-washing until the last moment before she left the bathroom in the morning. She washed her genitals in the shower and did not wash her hands when she came out.

The sessions were typically devoted to her describing how things went the previous week with the situations for which she had contracted. Her anxiety never reached panic proportions; it got high at times, but never over 60 degrees s.u.d.s (subjective units of disturbance). She couldn't understand why she didn't get more anxious. When her anxiety came she told herself it would pass. She felt I was there ''psychologically'' all the time. The thought of giving in and decontaminating herself became very aversive since she would have to face me the following week. The Benson's Relaxation Exercise helped a great deal in reducing her stress. The thought that she would be able to do it provided her with a sense of control over her anxiety when it came; she felt less helpless and vulnerable to the feelings consequent to not performing the anxiety-relieving rituals. She would tell herself that she would have the opportunity later to reduce her anxiety in the 20-minute period she had set aside. She did something else that was very useful in coping with the stress; after she had performed a particular act, like touching the doorknob of her front door, she not only prevented herself from decontamination but also immediately went on with her normal routine. In the case of the front doorknob she immediately went out of the house. She still felt the flooding effect of the anxiety as she walked to her car, but it became more tolerable.

I expected she would have some failures along the way, but I did not share this expectation with her. About six weeks into this period she decided that she would touch the lower part of her body, her legs and her hips, while she was in my office. It should be noted that this item (number 16) represented a leap in her progression through the hierarchical list. She had not as yet dealt with the two items, 14 and 15, that were directly sexual in nature. I felt she was probably avoiding these but I would return to them at a later period. We arranged for her to do item 16 the week that her husband would be home when she got there after her session with me. She could therefore have the benefit of his support when she got home. We decided that she would perform this most difficult act toward the end of the session in my office. She became visibly very anxious after having touched herself in my presence—she said her anxiety was around 90 s.u.d.s. I gave her considerable support, but her anxiety was still high when she left. The next week she reported that her anxiety was still high when she got home, after a 30-minute drive, and her husband wasn't there. He must have forgotten about their arrangement to be at home. She ran to the bathroom and immediately took a shower to decontaminate herself.

The following week we explored what had happened. We looked at the relevant events as processes that needed to be identified. Her thoughts and feelings constituted one part of the field of relevant events. She described these. She was quite anxious when she left my office. Surprisingly, in contrast to the previous behaviors she had attempted, her anxiety did not go down over the 30 minutes she was in the car on the way home. She was looking forward to the relief she would get when she arrived home and talked to her husband. When she didn't find him there, she went into a rage and felt fully justified in breaking the contract with me.

Her husband's not being there was an obvious critical external event that partially accounted for the patient's inability to prevent herself from performing the decontamination ritual. But why didn't her anxiety decrease on the way home? Theoretically, the nonreinforcement of her anxiety reaction through the prevention of the escape behavior (the decontamination ritual), should have resulted in an extinction effect. I speculated out loud that what must have happened was that the anticipation of seeing her husband and getting "relief" from him through his emotional support served, in this instance, the same function as the decontamination response. Her thoughts of his being home when she got there served as a negatively reinforcing function to the anxiety she was experiencing and thereby maintained it. In other words, in contrast to our plan to have her husband serve a desensitizing function in the sense of being a reciprocally inhibiting agent, he was experienced instead as a vehicle of escape from anxiety. When that expectation was frustrated, her anxiety increased even further. She felt overwhelmed and resorted to reducing her anxiety in the way she knew always worked.

We decided to test out this hypothesis during that session. I suggested she touch her legs in my presence and I would remain with her for the remainder of the session. If my analysis was correct, her anxiety would dissipate over that period of time since my presence, in contrast to that of her husband, would serve to provide her with the external control to prevent her from "escaping" through the performance of a decontamination ritual. My presence also would serve as a reassuring function to aid her in tolerating the anxiety she would experience.

She agreed that the strategy I outlined made sense. She touched her legs. Her anxiety level rose immediately, but not nearly as high as it had the week before. In about 30 minutes it was all over. She felt little or no anxiety. I instructed her to touch herself again and to keep her hands on her hips this time. Her anxiety went up again, but not as high as before. In another ten minutes it was down again. I instructed her to do this at home each day for at least a half hour. The following week she reported that this item on her list no longer presented a problem for her.

The psychodynamically oriented reader may wonder at this juncture about the patient's "transference" of sexual feelings to the therapist. What was described above was a situation where the patient, in touching her legs and her hips, assumed a sexual posture in the presence of the therapist. The concomitant arousal of sexual feelings in the patient could be presumed to be the "cause" of her anxiety. Certainly the history of the origin of the decontamination phobia in this patient—its association with anxious feelings accompanying menstruation—and others would support this hypothesis.

I did not test this hypothesis by inviting the patient to talk about what "feelings" she might be experiencing during this response prevention session in my office. There was no doubt that she was aroused sexually in my presence in this and in other sessions when a sexual history was taken. The sharing of intimate details of her sexual encounters with her husband were offered when not solicited by the therapist. She also became seductive at times through body movements, swinging her hips as she changed her position in her chair, etc. I dealt with these situations by not attending to the sexual messages being transmitted while remaining supportive and caring. Her seductiveness and the concomitant anxiety decreased in frequency until it was, in the end, extinguished. In other words, the "transference" itself was managed through the "response prevention" technique. The patient's covert seductive behavior "extinguished" in the absence of "reinforcement" from the therapist. So did her anxiety about the situation. The same "response exposure-response prevention" paradigm employed in dealing with her fear of contamination stimulated by touching her body, doorknobs, and other items, also served to manage the "transference" of sexual feelings to the therapist.

SESSIONS 14, 15, AND 16

I decided after this dramatic session to "coast" for awhile and not to take up any new behavioral changes. I did not want to overload her system. We had done a lot, I thought, so that I spent the subsequent three sessions talking with her about her week and monitoring the maintenance of the changes that had already occurred. I merely listened to her describe her day-by-day experiences during the previous week and supported her continuing successful attempts to desist from decontaminating after performing the previously contracted changes. Mrs. Collingsworth, however, began to spontaneously report on changes in some behaviors she had listed that were not yet directly contracted. She found herself, for example, going to the bathroom three or four times during her working day without any discomfort. She washed her hands once each time and walked out. She also reported in a matter-of-fact manner that she changed her kotex after menstruation without being compelled to engage in her usual ritualistic decontamination washing. This I knew was a significant gain, given the history of the origin of her contamination fear. She also reported on an equally impressive change. Previously she would invariably become constipated during her period of menstruation, presumably because of the tension associated with the accompanying fears of being contaminated. This now ceased to be the case.

It seemed to me at this point that it was time to deal with those items on her hierarchy that were more directly sexual in nature, namely 14 and 15. These have to do with her compulsion to decontaminate herself before and after having sex with her husband because she had touched the lower part of his body. I talked to her about this feeling of mine. She disagreed. She said she thought she was ready to tackle instead the most difficult issue which she had placed in the last, and so most feared, position in her hierarchy—touching the faucet in the bathroom and kitchen after she changed her kotex. She argued that since she felt ready now for what was to her an awesome undertaking, we ought not to detract from it by working on the sexual behaviors. I told myself that she was avoiding the sexual issues; when I shared this with her she laughed and said that she thought I was wrong. We decided to proceed with the "touching the faucet in the bathroom and kitchen" item. I reasoned that if she were avoiding the sexual items, this would become evident later and we would deal with it then. Furthermore, while she progressed through the hierarchy she did not do so in an orderly fashion. She skipped easier for more difficult items before and this did not retard her progress. It also seemed to me that this was a way she had of reducing her fear of being controlled by me. She made independent choices as to the next move and I supported these. It was agreed, then, that her contract for the next week was to touch the faucets in the bathroom and in the kitchen after she had changed her kotex. The next week she reported, in an almost matter-of-fact manner, that she had fulfilled the contract. It was, she said with more than a tinge of disappointment in her voice, unbelievably anticlimactic. The behavior she feared the most performing, and which she placed last on her hierarchy, aroused the least amount of anxiety. I explained that the "generalization" effect of having desensitized herself to the other items on the hierarchy decreased her level of arousal to similar behaviors.

THE NEXT 12 SESSIONS

We both agreed it was now time to deal with the two sexual items on the hierarchy, i.e., 14 and 15. Item 14 involved decontaminating by washing her genital area just before having sex with her husband at night. Item 15 was essentially an extension of number 14: she washed herself immediately after having sex with her husband. In addressing the sexual issue directly through a focus on these two related decontamination rituals, we initiated what, in fact, was a new phase of the treatment. This final phase required an additional 12 sessions over three months. It included, but was not limited to, the response prevention procedure which was the main technique used in the extinction of the decontamination rituals associated with the other items on her hierarchy. The treatment strategy was now expanded to include conjoint meetings with her husband, the employment of sexual retraining procedures, and the identification of a drinking problem she and her husband shared and which was related to the sexual inhibitions that prevented them from enjoying a full sexual life. The alcohol abuse problem was addressed concurrently with the sexual retraining that was instituted.

Again, the course of treatment in this final phase did not proceed in an orderly, systematic fashion. In fact, by the time we met again, Mrs. Collingsworth expressed a good deal of anger toward me. She was "fuming," she said, for a whole week. She was not very articulate about why she was angry. She mumbled something about an invasion of privacy. She knew I'd get around to focusing on her sex life with her husband and she did not like it. I became aware then how effective this patient had been up to this point in warding off any discussion and clarification of the sexual issues in her life. I had not been able, for example, to get a good sexual history—she had given me clear messages that this was too disturbing a topic for her. She was intending, now, to maintain this avoidance posture and her expressed anger toward me was an obvious way through which she hoped to detract me from pursuing this topic. I dealt with her anger by empathizing with the discomfort she felt by this line of inquiry. This was not an easy subject for many people to talk about; however it was necessary to do so in order to clarify issues and to plan intelligently the next phase of treatment. I said that, furthermore, I thought we ought to postpone instituting the response prevention procedure until I had had an opportunity to better understand the nature of her sexual relationship with her husband. She relaxed. I thought to myself that a kind of tradeoff had been negotiated without our labeling it as such. While she gave me the sexual history I said was important, she could enjoy a temporary moratorium from the response prevention procedure and the pain it involved.

I began by inquiring into her current sexual patterns. She and her husband had sex on the average of once a month. I reminded her she had told me, when I first took a history in the initial session, that she had sex twice a month. She said it varied from month to month, but that it was more like once rather than twice a month. This coincided with the days in her cycle when she was infertile. Her husband, Ralph, used a condom. Why had they not considered other contraception methods? Well, she told me, she had been planning to have an I.U.D. inserted but somehow never got around to seeing her gynecologist about this. Yes, she was satisfied with the frequency of sexual relations and so was her husband. Their views about not having children had not changed over the period during which she had been seeing me, in spite of the significant decrease of her compulsive decontamination rituals. I asked her then to detail again for me her daily activities, this time on an hourly basis. I wanted to understand better the general lifestyle that she and her husband lived. It was in response to this request that Mrs. Collingsworth revealed to me, for the first time, that she and her husband had been drinking excessively. She did not directly label herself or her husband as a problem drinker. Instead, she described a typical day as one in which she stopped after work and had two or three drinks with her coworkers at a local pub. When she arrived home she had another two or three drinks with her husband before dinner, then two drinks with dinner. After dinner they both enjoyed a ''couple'' of Southern Comforts. I wondered aloud how she felt about the amount of drinking she and her husband were doing. She knew, she said, that it was excessive and had consciously decided not to talk to me about it. Furthermore, she knew that drinking reduced her anxiety about the prospect of having sex. I said that alcohol was an inhibitor of sexual drives and that it could, in a negative feedback system way, be contributing to their having sex so infrequently; that is, anxiety about sex led to drinking to relieve the tension and effectively blocked the drive itself. The lack of sexual release probably increased the level of tension which led to more drinking, and added to the compulsive drive to decontaminate through washing.

It was on the basis of the above interpretation that dealing with the alcohol abuse problem became a legitimate target for behavior in the treatment. The patient did not directly request that her drinking behavior be addressed; she expressed no great distress about this. By hypothesizing its linkage to the decontamination rituals I suggested to her that it be included now in the treatment regimen.

Mrs. Collingsworth was not happy about this suggestion. She was even less happy when I told her in the next session that sexual retraining in the Masters and Johnson (1970) cast was also an indicated procedure that had to be part of a rounded therapeutic regimen. I also asked her to have her husband come in the following session so that the three of us could discuss this new course in the treatment, because his collaboration was essential.

Ralph Collingsworth is a tall, somewhat overweight person, dark-complected, and has an easy manner. There was a stubby growth on his chin suggesting he was in the early phase of growing a beard. He was shy and reticent in the interview room, and deferred often to his wife in the three-way interaction we were having. I asked him how he felt about his wife's progress. He said he was pleased; her previous therapist, he added, had been of no help at all. I asked him next whether his wife had discussed with him our last two sessions when we reviewed the sexual aspect of their lives and what I thought about their drinking in relation to this. He said she had not, in fact, done so. Mrs. Collingsworth giggled and demurely looked out the window. I briefly reviewed the course of Mrs. Collingsworth's treatment and the hypothesis concerning the effect of their drinking behavior on their sexual life. I also reviewed how I thought the decontamination behavior fit into the total picture. He agreed that it was a reasonable hypothesis. I outlined a three-pronged strategy that I wanted them to react to so that it could be adjusted in ways that could make it more effective.

The treatment plan I outlined was designed to focus on the three aspects of the negative feedback system: (1) Mrs. Collingsworth's contamination phobia in response to physical and sexual contact; (2) the sexual dysfunction in the marital relationship itself; and (3) the problematical drinking behavior.

The next block of sessions were conjoint ones in which the three "target" behaviors defined above were focused on as part of an integrated program for change. A detailed description of the implementation of the procedures employed in the treatment at this juncture will be provided below. Some clarifying statements about the posture of the therapist in implementing this therapeutic regimen is needed for a full understanding of how the therapy was conducted.

No systematic order was followed in dealing with the three aspects of the negative feedback system that bound them. I monitored the reactions of Mr. and Mrs. Collingsworth to the introduction of the different procedures and determined their tolerance level for both the specific changes being introduced and the rate at which these changes could take place. At times all three areas were worked on at once; at other times, the drinking problem or the sexual retraining procedures became the major focus. Concurrently, Mrs. Collingsworth maintained her previous therapeutic gains. She continued to resist engaging in decontamination rituals whenever urges to do so were stimulated by the situations identified and ordered on the original hierarchy.

The first issue I introduced was the need for Mrs. Collingsworth to consult her gynecologist about birth control measures. She said she would, but it took a total of four weekly reminders at the beginning of each session before she finally made an appointment and was subsequently fitted with a diaphragm.

Mrs. Collingsworth's fear of getting pregnant, it will be recalled, was related to her fear that a baby would be contaminated at birth by passing through an orifice that was "unclean." It made no sense to deal with her sexual inhibitions (and his) without her first feeling safe in regard to the fear of being impregnated. She was now able to say for the first time, following the visit to her gynecologist where she was measured for a diaphragm, that "Babies scare me . . . I don't want the responsibility." It became clearer now that Mrs. Collingsworth not only was fearful of sex, she was also fearful of assuming the adult motherhood role. This specific contamination phobia, in question then, served to make it possible for her to avoid the activation of anxiety that had broader origins than the sex act itself. Both the "immaturity" of Mrs. Collingsworth and that of her husband will be addressed later in this case analysis. The point that is being made now is that the focus on dealing with this specific contamination phobia through deconditioning, the sexual retraining, and the management of the drinking problem for both herself and her husband is not to be construed as ignoring the broader picture. In other words, what had already become quite evident was that these were two people with behavioral deficits beyond the sexual area itself. They had not, in their development, acquired a repertoire of behaviors necessary for an adult conjugal relationship. They were not only unprepared to invest in children, but in fact were unable to nurture each other sufficiently. The sexual dysfunction was a symptom of this "immaturity"; so was the problematical drinking that muted the anxiety they experienced when they confronted each other at the end of the work day. The intimacy was too much. It activated fears of engulfment by each other, so they contrived, in ways beyond their awareness, to avoid each other by drinking, as she did by her contamination phobias.

It was not in spite of, but because of the above formulation that a symptom focus was indicated. The reduction and elimination of these maladaptive behaviors had to precede the acquisition of more adaptive, "mature" ones. Once the specific symptoms were dealt with, the therapist's intention was to extend treatment so that the frequency of more adaptive and rewarding interpersonal interactions in the marriage might be increased. The use of Richard Stuart's (1969) format for accomplishing this was contemplated. At this juncture, however, the "target behaviors" isolated for attention had to be dealt with.

A critical first step was to review with Mr. Collingsworth, as I had done at the beginning of treatment with his wife, the concept of "contracting" as a necessary condition for our management of the problematic behaviors we had at this point agreed needed modification. This involved negotiations by the three of us as to which behaviors were to be broached, in what order and at what rate. Once we had agreed on what had to be done, I expected that the particular changes would have to be undertaken by them between sessions. A steady progression characterized by the elimination of undesirable behaviors and the acquisition of desirable ones constituted the basis of our continuing the treatment regimen. If they consistently failed to meet a contract they had participated in making, they, by definition, would have neutralized my ability to be of help to them. I was, here again, making my "love," i.e., support, conditional on their continued cooperation in the face of anticipated strong tendencies to avoid doing, or not doing, what previously had been a tension reducing, i.e., negatively reinforcing, act or acts.

Mr. Collingsworth got the point quickly. Incidentally, whatever issues of power and control had developed between them around sex could be expected in the context of this arrangement to be temporarily, at least, neutralized. I structured it so that, in my role as third party intervener, I became the locus of control, if only for a prescribed period of time.

The excessive drinking behavior was broached by my contracting with them to keep a written record over the ensuing week of what they drank, the amount they drank in ounces, the time of day, who else was present, and how they felt before and after each drinking period. I sensitized them to record especially their thoughts and feelings before and after they drank.

In this same session I explained in detail the rationale behind the Masters and Johnson (1970) sexual retraining method that we would be instituting at a later point.

The following session began with the report on their drinking behavior; they gave the daily account they had recorded at the end of each day. Their drinking patterns were similar in the amount they drank—averaging daily eight drinks of one and one-half ounces each. The beverages varied from beer to Manhattans, Southern Comfort, and wine. After work each of them had drinks with their colleagues and when they came home they had drinks together before dinner, usually hard liquor. During dinner they had beer or wine, after dinner Southern Comfort, and a nightcap (usually Southern Comfort again) before bed. This was the general pattern seven days a week. The most drinking took place on Friday night after a week of work was over.

They had remarkably little to report in regard to feelings and thoughts before or after they drank. Their drinking patterns had become almost ritualistic. They didn't think much about it before they drank and didn't report "feeling good" or "happy" during or after drinking. When urged to think about it by me, they conceded it must be tension-reducing or pleasurable since they drank so regularly.

I made a contract with them to reduce their daily intake by two drinks and to abstain entirely on one of the seven days, Thursday. In fact, they (primarily Mrs. Collingsworth) introduced this method after we had reviewed together various possible alternatives. They were to continue recording their daily intake and, now especially, any distress that was consequent to their reduction in alcohol intake.

Can you expect people to interrupt a long-standing habitual pattern by merely telling them to do so? Could this work? It can; it did work in this case, when certain conditions were met. First of all, motivation to stop was high; the drinking behavior, while long-standing, was not "out of control." They were both functioning productively in their jobs so that they had not reached an advanced stage of alcoholism. The firm external control in the form of the contracting method within the context of a strong therapeutic alliance, however, was the most important condition. They experienced the therapist as allied with them and they were heavily invested in meeting his expectations. The maintenance of this therapeutic alliance was a very reinforcing condition in their lives and they did not want to violate it. Finally, they experienced their control in the process was real, their inputs into the negotiation process were carefully considered, and in fact they had contributed the principal elements in the design of the method that was finally implemented.

THE NEXT TEN SESSIONS

Over the next ten sessions, following this general approach, their alcohol intake was brought under control. Their intake was reduced to three drinks a day, on two days a week they drank no alcohol at all, and their after work drinking was eliminated entirely. I planned with each of them alternative pleasurable activities during this crucial time of the day.

The sexual retraining procedures were initiated concurrently during this final phase of treatment. In the second session I initially used the "sensory focusing" technique. They were instructed to allow time in the evening to be in bed together without any outside distractions. Each was to massage the other in nonerogenous parts of their bodies. Skin creams could be used, if they found this helpful. The notion was to experience sensual feelings in a relaxed situation and without the condition that they perform coitus. Mrs. Collingsworth said she loved back rubs and could rarely get her husband to give her one. Mr. Collingsworth's shyness about physical contact became very apparent now, as we began a sequence of progressive steps that over the next few weeks would lead to sexual intercourse. He didn't say too much and wondered aloud if it made sense to proceed in this manner, but agreed to go along with it.

It took three weeks of "sensory focusing" before they were ready to move to the next step involving the stimulation of erogenous zones. The steps after that, undertaken in subsequent weeks, were foreplay, partial penetration, full penetration, and finally maintaining full penetration to the point of orgasm. Coitus was to be postponed until the time of the final step was agreed upon. The rationale behind this technique is the gradual disinhibiting of the sexual response by stimulating strong erotic feelings without the inhibiting conditions that each of them has to "perform" until they are both "ready." Theoretically, under these conditions the stimulated erotic feelings neutralize the anxiety that inhibits the sexual process from proceeding to its natural consummation.

The second step in this sequence was approached by Mrs. Collingsworth with less enthusiasm than the first. Touching her husband's body in the genital area activated the need to decontaminate herself by immediately getting out of bed and washing herself. She anticipated correctly that I would suggest this was an appropriate time to deal with this final item on her list of contamination phobias. She raised a serious objection. How could I expect them to proceed through the Masters and Johnson (1970) steps if she was burdened by the anxiety of not being able to decontaminate? I agreed that this was logical, but we ought to take an empirical "trial and error" posture and see what happened. She agreed reluctantly. The next week she reported mixed results. She touched her husband "below the waist" on one of the nights. She did not wash. She barely could fall asleep from the anxiety that came in waves. She awoke the next morning exhausted. The hand she used to touch her husband still felt "heavy"; her anxiety, although muted, still persisted so she rushed to the bathroom and washed her hands. She did not try "that" again for the rest of the week.

I empathized with her pain and pointed out the successful aspects of her effort, principally that she was able to withhold washing until the next morning. I also encouraged her to try it again the following week to see whether she could complete the process by waiting to wash until she took her morning shower. She agreed. I reinforced her for her tenaciousness and capacity to endure the pain involved. In this manner, I focused her attention on my expectation that she persevere the next time. It took two more weeks of daily "trying" until she finally succeeded. She was by now actually enjoying being stimulated by her husband in the genital area and twice had achieved orgasm in that manner. She said they hadn't planned on it, but found they were enjoying mutual masturbation. She was amazed that she could go to sleep without cleaning herself after these encounters.

By the end of this ten-week phase of treatment, the Collingsworths were having full intercourse at least three times a week. Mr. Collingsworth reported, in his usual impassive manner, that it was the best sex he ever had.

What had also become evident to me over this period were the behavioral deficits both had brought to their marriage from the early conditioning in their respective families. They were unable to fully "nurture" each other and, while the sex was now gratifying, I could not observe any change in their "supportive" relationship to each other. Mr. Collingsworth, for example, never offered to help his wife with supportive verbal and nonverbal communications while she went through the agonies of preventing herself from decontamination after touching him in the genital area. When they stopped drinking with each other, other activities were not engaged in conjointly.

I suggested strongly that we now work on these interpersonal issues and began to describe a potential treatment plan based on Stuart's (1969) methods. Mrs. Collingsworth took a strong stand at this point. She got what she came for, she said, and they did not want to continue treatment at this time. I persisted and recommended they seek out another therapist who was a specialist in marital therapy. Mr. Collingsworth said nothing. Mrs. Collingsworth remained adamant. She again said that she was grateful for all I had done for them but she did not want to continue with anyone.

What had emerged, furthermore, in this last phase of treatment was the power imbalance in their relationship. She obviously was, and planned to remain, the dominant partner in their relationship. I worried about how they would now redefine their relationship in the absence of her phobias and the reduction of their drinking. They did not share these concerns when I verbalized them. They also agreed with each other that things were fine enough between them and they felt they could deal with their marital issues when they would come up "by themselves."

I made two follow up telephone calls, one a year later and the second a year after the first. The treatment of her phobias held quite well and there was no serious regression. Urges to decontaminate would occur from time to time, but were of manageable intensity. On occasion she gave in and decontaminated, but this did not result in a snowballing effect. She did not take these "failures" seriously. Mostly, she was symptom free.

Her relationship with her husband? On this point she was more vague. Good days and bad days, she said, in what seemed to me a defensive posture. Sexual relations remained good. They had planned to have a baby; in fact she got pregnant, but had a miscarriage.

I could not determine from these calls what was happening in their marital relationship. The power issue, I felt, had not been dealt with and so there remained an endemic source of strain. I speculated how the removal of her symptoms and the amelioration of their sexual dysfunction would effect this balance. I knew that an important aspect of their relationship had to have changed by the therapy—that is, the negatively reinforcing function that they served for each other, or in other words, the mutual dependency that allowed each of them to support the other in avoiding life situations that made them anxious.

8

A Case History of a Man Whose Functioning Was Impaired by Severe Anxiety Attacks

This case was selected because it makes it possible to illustrate the behavioral treatment of acute anxiety where both cultural and individual conditioning factors were of central importance. These factors were taken into account in both the behavioral analysis and the treatment-planning phases of the therapy. This is the case of a Greek-American man, then 24 years of age, who was entrapped in a system of relationships that were patterned by cultural expectations of how he should think, feel, and act. These Greek-cultural expectations (Papajohn & Spiegel, 1975) tended to reinforce the irrational demands of a widowed woman who maintained his anxiety by overprotecting him. The consequent fear of entrapment fueled his efforts to separate from her and to individuate. Movement away from her, however, resulted in severe fears of abandonment which took the form of acute anxiety attacks.

Bill Anastos was referred to me by a psychiatrist who told me that he thought of me as the "ideal" therapist for this man on two different bases. The first was that he needed behavioral treatment for a specific fear, principally the severe anxiety that hampered his performance in a job interview situation and secondly, because we shared a common cultural background. He had treated him over the previous two years psychodynamically. Actually he had also treated him three years earlier when he was a student at a local university. He had seen him then on and off for about a year because of acute disabling anxiety around exam time. A combination of support and antianxiety medication served to get him over these crises. He was not ready for more intensive psychotherapeutic work until he graduated from college two years before.

They had done a great deal of "reconstructive" work together, having explored his early relationship to his Greek-born mother and to his father, who had died when the patient was 13 years old. What persisted, the psychiatrist said, was a residual fear of taking job interviews. His patient, in fact, was leaving Boston in about three weeks and he wondered whether I would be willing to do some focused work on this specific "phobia." He was planning to join his older brother and his married sister who had moved to a large city in the western part of the country. In fact, his brother had already set up some job interviews for him there. The patient was apprehensive about these. Could I do some "systematic desensitization or something" to help him with his fear of taking interviews?

I told the psychiatrist that I could not, since there was no time for a behavioral analysis and so treating this symptom in a kind of psychological vacuum would probably be a futile effort. The psychiatrist said that he was sure he could prevail on his patient to remain in the Boston area a little longer if I needed more than three weeks. I told myself that I could at least prepare this patient for continued behavior therapy in the city to where he was moving. In fact, a colleague I knew well was practicing there and I could refer Bill Anastos to him if it seemed appropriate and if he wanted to continue. Also, I probably could help him, even if only symptomatically, to get through the immediate situation that was confronting him.

THE INITIAL INTERVIEW

Bill Anastos was early for his first session with me. He is a tall man, who appeared to be somewhat underweight, and is dark-complected with brown eyes. He wore dark-rimmed glasses. What impressed me most was the almost childlike, wide-eyed passivity that characterized his manner of relating to me. He was 24 years old. He hung on my every word. He told me right off that he arranged to postpone his moving to the west coast for a month. That gave us a total of two months, eight sessions, to focus on the problem he wanted help with—his anxiety in job interview situations. He could not come twice a week. I began with a functional analysis of the presenting problem or symptom. In this process of identifying the precipitating factors for the onset of panic and clarifying his reactions in the job interview situations, I was also able to take a brief history and to initiate him into a behavioral way of conceptualizing his difficulties. By the end of this first session, which lasted a full 60 minutes, I was also able to introduce some techniques for managing his anxiety.

I asked him to describe the most recent incident of experiencing anxiety in an interview. About six months before, he had applied for a job in a major Boston department store chain. He was a college graduate with a major in liberal arts and wanted specifically to be trained for a position in management. He had submitted a written application for the management training program that this department store corporation provided. He received a phone call from the secretary who proceeded to discuss some possible times that he could meet with the personnel director, who was interviewing all the eligible candidates for these training positions. Bill's anxiety began to rise in the course of this telephone conversation. He had obviously passed the first test of eligibility and would now be evaluated in a more concentrated way. This was only a flitting thought during the conversation, but during the following week his anxiety level progressively mounted. He felt anxious whenever he thought of the interview date getting closer and closer, day by day, hour by hour. The thought that he would soon have to appear at the personnel office and be interviewed would pop into his head intermittently throughout the week and anxiety would "rush in." These were specific thoughts of being evaluated and failing. It was simply, he said, the image of himself in the interview situation that would trigger the anxiety. The night before the interview he slept very little. He found himself drinking scotch after supper in an effort to calm himself. He managed to fall asleep and awoke in the morning with a deep sense of impending doom. This feeling persisted during breakfast and on his way to the interview. He almost rammed into the rear of a car that had stopped ahead of him for a red light. He was greeted cordially by a secretary who asked him to wait in a reception area. He sat down, barely able to contain the trembling that now caused his legs and arms to shake. The thought that this shaking might be noticed by the other people in the reception area intensified his feeling of panic. After waiting for ten minutes, he said that he was sure he was going to die, so overwhelming had his anxiety become. He had to get out of there at all costs. He got up and bolted from the building.

Bill wanted to be sure that I understood how intense his anxiety had been in that situation. I assured him that I got the idea. Since that incident he has been unable to even "think" of applying for another job. The words "help wanted" in the employment section of the newspaper were enough to trigger his anxiety. He therefore worried about what would happen when he got to California. I told him that I would help him learn ways of managing his anxiety. I inserted here the notion that the intense anxiety he had described could be brought under control through learning to substitute alternative relaxation reactions to the same situations. Bill could only hear this dimly. I am sure what was more reassuring was the feeling I transmitted that his was a familiar condition which I had treated before and that I felt confident I could be of help. He visibly relaxed. I told him I would begin in today's session to teach him some relaxation techniques, but that I needed first to familiarize myself with his background. I explored, through a succession of direct questions, the conditions of his life. I began with the present. I decided to first take a horizontal view of his current life situation and postpone a more "in depth" inquiry into his presenting problem for a later session.

Bill was currently employed by his uncle (that is, his mother's sister's husband), who owned a large and successful restaurant on the south shore. He had worked there summers during his college years, and for the two years since graduation. He started out as a busboy, worked up to a waiter, and for the last year was promoted to maître d. He made good money at this job and his uncle, who was getting old, implied from time to time that should he agree to remain permanently he would make him a partner in the business. Bill was tempted. He felt comfortable in this work environment. Most of the waiters and chefs were Greek or Greek-American and he was treated with respect there. He was accepted because he was one of them, a clansman and a member of their cultural in-group, as well as the nephew of the boss. He was supported (i.e., reinforced) just by virtue of who he was, rather than solely by what he achieved in his work. This was consistent with the Greek norms of culture that patterned relationships in the family in which he grew up. His job situation then constituted an extension of his Greek family. It provided an accepting supportive environment and shielded him from the stresses incumbent in "making it" occupationally and socially in the broader "American" social system.

Bill, however, had been socialized in two cultures. He had also learned to value achievement in American middle-class terms. He could not remain contented, as a college graduate, in his role of maître d at his uncle's restaurant. This was not a job commensurate with his education. Furthermore, and this made things even more confusing, he was aware that upward social mobility and individual achievement were also highly valued goals in his subculture. One was accepted because they were Greek, but they were also expected to achieve because they were Greek. Bill's peers had all gone to college and were highly successful in their different professions. Obviously, Bill could not relax. He was buffeted by conflicting expectations of how he should think and what he should do.

What fueled this conflict, I thought, was the symbiotic relationship he had with his mother. He had clearly been the "man of the house" since his father's death. He lived with her in the house she grew up in and she depended on him for the satisfaction of a broad range of emotional needs. She cooked for him, they went to church together, he called when he expected to be out late, and he did the repairs on the house. She never even came close to developing a relationship with another man since her husband's death 11 years before. She was 41 years old when he died. Bill did have a girlfriend he had been seeing since his senior year in college. At the time it was a relationship of three years duration. Connie worked as a bank teller in town. It was a "full" relationship. The sexual part was "good." She had never met his mother. He seemed bewildered by the surprise that I registered when he told me this; he never thought much about it, he said. His mother knew who she was and never said anything disapproving about the matter. He guessed, now that I forced him to think about it, that he kept these two aspects of his life separate. It was clear to me, if not to Bill, that he and his mother had colluded in a covert agreement to make this woman, Connie, a nonperson who would not disrupt their mutually dependent relationship. I did not share this interpretation with Bill. Also, it didn't surprise me that Connie wasn't Greek, since she was not considered to be a real marriage prospect. I knew that in Greek culture non-Greek women were considered to be suspect and that all Greek women by definition were acceptable. In this case, this was not an issue. The question of marriage itself was a nonissue in the context of the characteristics of Bill's relationship with his mother. She recognized that he had sexual needs which had to be met outside the home, and also emotional needs which she herself was determined to meet within the home.

By the end of this first session, I felt that I had established sufficiently good rapport with Bill to be able to begin setting up contracts with him. I felt comfortable with the directive posture I had assumed with him. It was a posture that was familiar to him, since he grew up in a home where relationship was ordered on a hierarchical (i.e., lineal) basis. That is to say, Bill had learned to respect authority. I also sensed that this "transference" phenomenon had to be handled carefully since Bill was also more than ready to develop a passive, dependent relationship with me, not to mention the concomitant resistance that could accompany this. The management of the "transference" was greatly enhanced by my understanding of Greek culture (Spiegel, 1971, Chap. 10). I knew that in Greek homes a son's pathway to individuation is patterned by a different set of expectations or "value orientations" than in American middle-class culture. The father assumes an authoritarian posture toward the son, who behaves in ways that acknowledge his "right" to do so. The son respects his father's ability to "take over" and to guide and protect the members of his family in a firm, self-confident, and effective manner. In return for the acceptance of his father's position as head of the household, the son receives his unwavering support—emotional, financial, and other. There are no limits. Furthermore, the son's own independence is attained by modeling (i.e., identifying with) the father's strength. He continues to show respect toward his father throughout adolescence, early adulthood, middle age, and especially when his father's physical and mental powers begin to wane. In "healthy" families love and respect toward the father become indistinguishable (Papajohn & Spiegel, 1975).

This pattern is to be contrasted with that of American culture where individuation is predicated on the rejection of all authority during adolescence. This rejection becomes the basis on which the redefinition of oneself as an independent individual, who then becomes free to love, is predicated. Bill was subject to these two contrasting sets of socializing experiences. His personal experience was further complicated by his father's death when he was an adolescent. To complicate things further, I was to learn later that his father and mother had a poor marital relationship—they were locked in a struggle for power and control in the family. This struggle was, in part, due to the acculturation process the family was going through in the transition from Greek to American ways of thinking, feeling, and acting, (i.e., value orientations) that caused confusion between the husband and wife in the areas of role definition, decision making, and so forth. I will elaborate on this point later.

I taught him Benson's Relaxation Response and contracted with him to practice it twice a day. I also prepared him for "cognitive restructuring" by talking briefly about the fact that his anxiety was triggered by catastrophizing thoughts. I told him that I wanted him also to write down at the end of each day the thoughts that he had before and during those periods when he felt anxious. He readily agreed to do so.

THE NEXT SEVEN SESSIONS

I had crammed a lot of the behavioral analysis in the first session and felt that I had to rely on the data I was able to obtain to design a treatment strategy. In fact, given the narrow time frame that I had to work in, I also had to rely on impressions inferred from the facts I obtained to guide me in deciding on how to approach the presenting problem.

Bill reported that he did Benson's Relaxation Response twice a day during the past week and that it had "somewhat" of a calming effect on him. Yes, he also monitored his behavior and noticed that he felt anxious whenever he thought of taking a job interview. He felt a low level of anxiety "all the time," except when he was working or when he was with his girlfriend, Connie. It seemed to him that he was more tense when he was home with his mother, but he was not sure about this.

I decided to start with systematic "desensitization." The reason I chose to begin with this technique was somewhat arbitrary. It is a relatively nonthreatening procedure for most patients and so I like to begin with it; this is especially important when the opportunity is not present for a thorough behavioral analysis, in which a patient's tolerance for anxiety can be assessed. It also provides a means for the patient to experience the effectiveness of behavioral procedures in controlling the anxiety response. Systematic desensitization is also a paradigm of the general behavioral approach to managing anxiety because it brings into sharp relief the principle of gradual exposure to conditions that evoke it as the condition for its progressive extinction.

I again reviewed with Bill the notion that anxiety is learned and so can be unlearned following the same principles of association. He understood. First we had to develop a hierarchy of situations in which he was anxious that were related to a job interview. These were ordered on a scale that reflected progressively higher levels of potential for eliciting anxiety. We constructed a seven-step hierarchy through a series of my inquiries. This was a two-way process in which I asked him to think of what specific situations elicited what amounts of anxiety (rated on a subjective scale of 0–100). The following seven items constituted the final scale. They are ordered from least to most anxiety-provoking:

1. Reading the help wanted section of the Sunday newspaper
2. Receiving a phone call from a prospective employer
3. The evening before the day of the interview
4. The morning of the day of the interview
5. Waiting in the reception room for the interview to start
6. Being introduced to the interviewer
7. Sitting in the interviewer's office and attempting to formulate a response to a question that was asked.

I next did imagery training with Bill. I started with a neutral scene. I asked him to close his eyes and imagine sitting in his living room at home. "Construct the scene, gradually focusing on one item at a time," I told him. "When you focus on the couch, for example, include the color, texture, and size. Feel the proprioceptive cues when you focus on experiencing sitting in the arm chair. Employ all the sensory modalities you can to make the scene as real as possible, including smells. Experience being there rather than looking 'in on' the scene." I stopped giving instructions and after three or four minutes I asked him to rate the quality of the scene he constructed on a scale of 0–5, with 5 representing really feeling he is there and 0 no approximation to the real situation. Bill got it quickly. He was able to imagine the scene readily.

I next asked him to do the same with the first item on his hierarchy. First, however, I wanted him to relax for a couple of minutes through employing Benson's Relaxation Response. When doing this and his anxiety level was reduced to 15 s.u.d.s (subjective units of disturbance) or lower, he was to raise the forefinger of his right hand. After Bill relaxed in this manner, I instructed him to turn on the scene of the first (least anxiety-evoking) item on his hierarchy. He signaled he had done this. I next asked him to raise his forefinger when he felt anxiety imagining this scene. When he did so I started a silent timer and waited for 25 seconds. I then asked him to turn off the scene and to turn on Benson's Relaxation Response. When his anxiety had returned to a 15 s.u.d.s level he was to indicate this by raising his forefinger. This sequence constituted a single trial of systematic desensitization procedure.

I asked Bill to practice this procedure at home and immediately after he did the Benson's Relaxation Response. He was to spend approximately 20 minutes twice a day at this. During each practice session he was to get in as many trials as he could. He was not to move to item 2 on his hierarchy until he reached the point where the configuration of stimuli that constituted scene 1 no longer elicited any anxiety; in other words, when experiencing this scene left him feeling relaxed and peaceful.

Bill reported the following week that he averaged 15 trials per session and that after three days or six sessions he moved onto scene 2 of his hierarchy and, in fact, had been desensitized to that scene as well.

I had begun this third meeting by first asking Bill how things had gone during the week. He reported feeling much calmer in general and then described the experience he had with systematic desensitization. He was still considerably apprehensive, however, about his trip to the west coast and the job interviews that awaited him there. I wondered out loud how much of his anxiety was caused by the anticipated interviews and how much by the separation he would have to experience in moving to another part of the country. He said separations were always a problem for him. He remembered the extreme anxiety he experienced when at the age of ten he was sent to camp; it was more like dread that never got better and after two days his mother coming to get him. Going to college was traumatic. It was better than the camp situation, but he never really adjusted; that is, he never felt totally relaxed there. Later on, having a steady girlfriend, Connie, helped a great deal. He didn't think that was the major issue now, however, since his brother and sister were there and his mother planned to precede him.

We refocused on our current anxiety management effort. I told him to continue the systematic desensitization procedure at home and to work his way up the hierarchy of items. I would monitor his progress each week in the office. Concurrently I wanted him to locate, through the newspaper, at least three job situations for which he theoretically qualified and to procure and send in the required applications. He was to set up interviews, if he could, for the week before he was to leave for the west coast. He should arrange for at least three such interviews. These interviews would constitute *in vivo* (real life) experiences that would be incorporated into our desensitization effort. By experiencing these different stages leading to actual interviews while concurrently desensitizing them in imagination, he would have the advantage of a kind of double exposure and both in a controlled manner. This approach should maximize the anxiety response extinction process. He understood. My support and direction constituted, of course, an additional desensitization effect that complemented the *in vivo* and the *in vitro* (in imagination) experiences. This was a "transference" effect, with which I, in the role of the supportive but directive Greek father, complemented the procedures that were employed.

In this session I also introduced the behavioral rehearsal procedure that, as will be evident, enhanced even further the desensitization process incorporated in the procedures already described. I asked him to prepare for our next therapy sessions a series of questions of the kind he anticipated to be asked in the interview situations. He was to read these questions out loud to himself and to respond with what he considered to be appropriate answers.

In the following (fourth) session, Bill brought the questions in and I set up a simulated interview situation in the office. I took the role of interviewer and asked Bill to respond to the questions he had prepared. This experience was an especially poignant one for Bill. He became visibly anxious after the second question and said he couldn't continue. I asked him to tell me what he was feeling. He said he felt like he was tied up and placed on railroad tracks and a train was approaching and he couldn't get free. He felt, he said, as he might in the real interview situation—as if he was in too far and was losing control. Bill's graphic description of anxiety was not commensurate with what I was observing his distress to actually be. His cognition and his affect were disparate regarding the degree of disorganization that they manifested. I did not share this perception with Bill. I suggested that we stop the behavioral rehearsal for the time being. I asked him to close his eyes, do Benson's Relaxation Response, and raise his forefinger when he was relaxed; he did so after about three or four minutes. I shifted the focus to asking him how the systematic desensitization had gone the previous week. He was up to item 5: Waiting in the reception room for the interview to start. This item still needed work. I told myself that I must be rushing things with the behavioral rehearsal, since it corresponded to the last item on his desensitization hierarchy (actually being in the interview situation itself). He obviously wasn't ready for this. I postponed this procedure and took it up again the following week. He had by then completed the last item on the hierarchy and the behavioral rehearsal went more smoothly. I am not sure whether, indeed, there was a causal connection between the systematic desensitization and his ability to do the behavioral rehearsal. Other desensitization experiences like Benson's Relaxation Response or the "transference effect" may have accounted for the difference. What is important is that he was, in general, more ready to take the job interviews he had set up in two (not three) of the companies he had applied to in the meantime. These were scheduled within a two-day period about one week before he was to leave for the west coast.

In the therapy session (the sixth) just prior to those job interviews, I employed a flooding technique which took up most of the hour. I felt Bill was ready for this. He had desensitized himself to the last scene where he was in the actual job interview situation. It had resulted in significant dimunition of anxiety, but he was still uneasy about facing the real situation itself. Until this point, furthermore, he did not have to anticipate the real situation as an immediate contingency. It was to take place in the future. The future, however, was now upon him and I think this is why more desensitization trials were required. I decided to try "flooding" because there was no time left for more protracted desensitization trials.

I instructed him to relax and to close his eyes. I explained the rationale undergirding this procedure first. I would try to create a scene in which he would experience high levels of anxiety. He was to assist me by guiding me in the process of constructing a scene so that it would be maximally anxiety-provoking for him. I explained the process of extinction through the use of the concept of "immunization" as a metaphor. The psychological system builds up antibodies to high levels of disorganizing anxiety; thereby one becomes immune. I told him to close his eyes and to clear his mind. I then asked him to imagine actually being in the interviewer's office and to include all the visual, auditory, and other stimuli or features of the scene. "Imagine the interview starting," I told him. "You hear the interviewer asking the initial question as he skims over your application form. You feel the anxiety rising as you did in the real situation you described to me in the initial therapy session. Now the perception of yourself being anxious, the visceral cues, cause you to be more anxious. Your anxiety is now interfering with your thinking. You can't organize a response to the question because your thoughts are not clear. The interviewer looks at you; he notices that you are anxious. You notice that he has noticed. Now your anxiety has reached panic proportions." Every minute or so I asked Bill to tell me, on a scale of 0–100 s.u.d.s, how much anxiety he was experiencing. He reported 75 s.u.d.s at this point. "Now you want to bolt out of the room but can't get off your seat. You feel utterly helpless and powerless. You actually start to sob. The interviewer is shocked. He makes some fumbling effort to be supportive," I said. Bill's anxiety, he reported, was now "over 100 s.u.d.s." "The interviewer opens the door and asks the secretary to come in. She sees you crying and starts to laugh. You feel even worse, like you're dying."

I instructed Bill to stay with that scene and to embellish it with details of his own in order to keep up the anxiety level. He nodded that he understood. I stopped talking. After about ten minutes, he signaled me by raising his forefinger that his anxiety was decreasing. It was now around 50 s.u.d.s. I told him to open his eyes when it went below 20 s.u.d.s. He did so after another five minutes.

Bill was remarkably relaxed after this flooding session. He told me he embellished the scene by imagining that as he is leaving the office crying, he meets people he knows in the street, and his helplessness is further exposed to ridicule.

Three days later, Bill took the two job interviews that he had previously scheduled in the Boston area. In the last (seventh) session, he described what happened in a casual, matter-of-fact manner that reflected the anticlimactic nature of the experience itself. He had some anxiety while waiting in the reception area and some in the interview situation itself just before they got started. The interviewer was especially nonthreatening, i.e., relaxed and casual. After Bill responded to the first question, what anxiety he had disappeared entirely.

We talked about his trip to the west coast. Once he got settled there, his mother planned to sell her house in the Boston area and move out there. She had flown out there the previous week to be with his brother and sister. He was leaving in a few days to join them. He was apprehensive about the move, but felt he could handle the interviews. I was not as confident as Bill about this. I felt that I had brought the most to bear on helping him to manage his anxiety in this situation; yet I was not confident about the stability of the gains we had made. I knew there was a great deal more work to be done in the other areas of love and work in his life. I sensed his vulnerability and his reliance on his family for support. I told myself that the mutual interdependencies he had with his mother, brother, and sister were consistent with the structure and function of roles in Greek families, and so not necessarily problematic. Yet, Bill lacked the confidence and self-assertion that is also present in Greek males who have been able to identify with a father.

Bill thanked me. No mention was made of contacting me again, nor was there expression of termination anxiety. It ended in a matter-of-fact, casual fashion.

THE NEXT PHASE OF TREATMENT

About five weeks later, Bill called me from the west coast. He was returning to Boston. Would I have time to see him? He sounded distressed.

When he appeared in my office, a week after his arrival in Boston, he looked tired. When he arrived at his sister's house on the west coast he found his mother, his brother and his wife, and his sister and her husband sitting around the dining room table waiting for him. He experienced a panic he could not understand. Did he feel entrapped by them? He didn't know; probably, he said. He was so anxious that he was not able to think of what could be causing it. He asked for a drink. He drank a lot that day and that night. He did not share his feelings with his family. His brother talked about the job interviews he had arranged for him the following week. This clearly fueled his anxiety and increased his rate of drinking. The following week he went to a total of six job interviews. They went surprisingly well. He took a job with a large food brokerage firm as a sales representative. Two weeks later, the first day on the job, he panicked. He had a full-blown anxiety attack. It started almost immediately after his arrival in the office. The boss chatted with him briefly and then turned him over to the regional sales manager, who began explaining to him what his functions would be. Bill had never worked in this field before; he had no frame of reference, he said, within which to process the information he was being given. That is what triggered his anxiety. Somehow he got through the day but never went back. His brother was really angry because he had made the contacts for him. His brother-in-law and sister were clearly disappointed but tried to be supportive. His mother worried out loud about his anxiety. She encouraged him not to take the job since it upset him so. This response of hers enraged him. He felt even more helpless. He continued to drink too much. He decided to take a vacation and spent the next couple of weeks just hanging around his sister's house and drinking. He drove home alone across the country. On the way, passing through a southern state, he was stopped for speeding. It was at night. He panicked when he saw the state trooper's red lights flashing behind him. He had visions of being murdered by red neck southerners. Then he called me.

In this session I listened and was supportive. I contracted with him to resume doing Benson's Relaxation Response, to reestablish social contacts in the Boston area, principally with his girlfriend, Connie, and to stop drinking. I noted, but did not pursue the fact, that little mention was made of Connie in this session. His intended separation from her when he left Boston was never raised as an issue, nor was any reference made to her until I asked. He said that he had seen her since he returned and, in fact, he had slept at her apartment a couple of nights. He hadn't terminated his relationship with her when he left and he had left it as it always was—undefined. He never said he would marry her, he told me, and she seemed to feel OK about the arrangement they had.

THE NEXT SIXTEEN SESSIONS

I resumed seeing Bill on a weekly basis. It would now be possible for me to complete the behavioral analysis and to set up some broader treatment goals.

This phase of treatment was characterized by a flow of complexly interrelated events, both within the therapeutic sessions and in Bill's interaction with his environment. I shall now present them as separate events to describe what went on in the therapy. Being part of the process itself, I was not fully cognizant of the subtleties of what was happening until this period of 16 sessions was over. The events that I am referring to are as follows: (1) furtherance of the behavioral analysis; (2) the reinstitution by me of techniques to help Bill manage his anxiety; (3) his efforts to move out and to procure a job in the Boston area; and (4) Bill's interactions with his mother. In the therapeutic sessions Bill picked up where he had left off before leaving for the west coast; but now he offered information about his background and his history in a more spontaneous, open manner. He focused a great deal on his mother. He had done a lot of this, he said, with his previous therapist. His mother had always been fearful of life in general. She constantly warned him to be careful of getting physically hurt when he was growing up. She told him not to be aggressive with people because they would turn on him. She encouraged him to avoid confronting difficult situations, such as problems with peers or finishing a task he had started, like building a model plane. When he studied a great deal she worried that he would get too tired. Things worsened after his father died. She became unbearably overprotective.

His contact with his father had been minimal. His father was part owner of a restaurant and worked constantly. Bill rarely saw him. His father did not get along well with his mother. He remembers being awakened at night by their arguing. The father drank a great deal. Bill remembered hearing his mother accuse him of going out with other women. This especially frightened him.

Bill was reestablishing his relationship with me. Previously he had given me information only in response to direct questioning; now he offered details of his relationship with his family in a more open manner. He was confiding in me. He was expressing his trust.

He said little about his siblings. His brother was five years older than he was and his sister was seven years older. They lived in separate worlds. They cared about him, but he never really felt close to them.

I knew that his mother's fearful stance in relation to life was partially culturally patterned. So was her overprotectiveness. She grew up in a rural area of Greece and had internalized an orientation to the physical and social environment that incorporated the belief and feeling that one is subject to the vagaries of life, and vulnerable to inimical forces beyond one's control. She shared this orientation with southern European rural people in general. This feeling must have been intensified when she emigrated with her parents to this urban society with all its real and imagined dangers. Her husband, Bill's father, for whatever reason could not provide her with the sense of safety and love she needed. He fought her when she tried to subvert his patriarchal position within the family. After his death, her early culturally conditioned fears of the world must have been exacerbated. She turned to her children and especially her youngest, Bill, for support. Greek widows do not remarry very easily. It is almost a betrayal of their family to do so. She had no occupation. She was dependent on her children for emotional survival. Bill was the one designated to provide her with what she needed and she meant to see to it that she was not cut off. In Greek families the youngest child is often designated as the one to take care of the parents in old age; or if one parent dies, the youngest child is expected to take care of the survivor.

It is important to emphasize here that Bill's mother's psychological deprivation and her feelings of helplessness and powerlessness were exacerbated by the stress of culture change. She was uprooted at the age of 11 from the rural village life in which she had been socialized. She was separated from grandparents, cousins, and other support persons to be thrust into a strange and confusing urban environment. She had to negotiate the developmental tasks of adolescence and sexual differentiation as part of a Greek family living in an Anglo-Saxon Protestant world. The expectations of how to think, feel, and act from two variant cultural sources compounded her sense of help-lessness and so lowered her threshold of fear of abandonment. Her husband's death must have been experienced by her as a totally catastrophic event. In the absence of other supports, such as a job and friends, she turned to her family, primarily Bill, in order to feel safe.

These cultural insights helped me to understand what Bill was up against. His "individuation" would have to almost literally be a life and death strug-gle. It turned out that I had not overestimated the enormity of the task of in-dividuation that confronted him. The symbiotic bond between them was very strong in both directions. It also became evident that Bill faced issues of ac-culturation, albeit in a muted form, that paralleled those of his mother. He, too, was torn between two culturally patterned sets of expectations, Greek and American. His individuation, i.e., confronting his anxiety about separa-tion and moving toward individualistic independent directions, involved issues of culture change. Breaking the symbiotic bond with his mother meant differentiating between mutually contradictory expectations of how he should think, feel, and act. A good son was defined by his mother to mean liv-ing with her, spending time with her, and maintaining a primary emotional tie to her that excluded others. The tradeoff was the feeling of safety his mother provided. By keeping him close to her, she shielded him from the anxiety in-cumbent in moving out to "American" ways in love and work. Movement toward assuming responsibility and behaving in independent ways in the oc-cupational area was accompanied by feelings of loneliness and the panic of feeling that he couldn't accomplish tasks. These feelings were followed by the anxiety that he would be judged negatively by an employer and fired. The final abandonment—Bill's vulnerability to feelings of rejection by authority figures—was, of course, traceable to the absence of a father. He had not learned appropriate male role behaviors in the context of a traditional Greek family structure where the father assumes the dominant role. Commitment to a woman, especially a non-Greek woman, meant a final emotional separation from his mother. He would be expected to perform, to take care of others, to be independent, and to be found wanting meant he would be cast out and so abandoned again.

Individuation for Bill, then, involved essentially a culture change process. He needed to extinguish the anxiety that would be activated by moving in "American" directions and to experience reinforcing effects of thinking, feeling, and acting in "individualistic" ways. This is how I processed Bill's efforts to move out into an occupation at this juncture of treatment. His anx-iety subsided significantly after I had seen him for two sessions, two days apart. At this point he had been in Boston for about three weeks. He drank only occasionally now, he said. He was ready to try again, and in fact he had located a possible job through a friend.

I supported Bill's determination to "try again" by pursuing an appropriate job. This was the obvious direction to go in furthering the individuation process. The major focus in this phase of treatment then became the management of Bill's anxiety as he moved out in the job market.

He made a job contact through a friend who was a "buyer" for a large department store chain. His friend suggested that Bill spend time with him during his work week to become familiar with what he did and to determine whether he indeed wanted to apply for a job with the same company. This seemed to me an ideal arrangement in that it provided for graduated exposure *in vivo* in the real situation to the anxiety-evoking events or stimuli that he would need to confront in taking this job. Bill agreed.

The first day he followed this man around as he made the rounds of department stores, identifying what merchandise needed replenishing and learning where and how to order it. Bill was in no way being judged at this point since he was, in a sense, merely an observer. He became anxious anyway. He was obsessed about the different operations his friend engaged in to carry out his job. He worried that he wouldn't be able to remember everything. He worried about his bosses, whom as yet he hadn't met. After two weeks of this "trial" period, he decided to apply for a job as a "buyer." His anxiety shot up the minute his friend agreed to set up an appointment for him to be interviewed by the regional manager.

He had been doing Benson's Relaxation Response. I introduced cognitive restructuring as a technique for counteracting the ruminative thoughts that plagued more persistently now. We practiced in the office. I asked him to close his eyes and to allow himself to think of an anxious thought related to his upcoming interview. He indicated by raising his forefinger that he had. I instructed him to now turn on the "prepared script" we had previously constructed together. The script read as follows: "I am quite capable of presenting myself in an effective manner to this man. This sense of helplessness and powerlessness is not related to the interview situation. I do not need to give in to it; I am not a victim of my past experiences."

The script varied, but it provided for a prepared set of reality oriented self-statements that were designed to counteract the unrealistic, anxiety-generating ones he had associated with situations in which he would be judged. I had prepared him for the cognitive restructuring technique by repeated inputs during the sessions in which I had elaborated the theme of conditioned thoughts, feelings, and actions. This was part of the behavioral orientation to his subjective experience of anxiety that I continually provided through my interpretations of the different events that he brought to me. In a sense, then, the cognitive restructuring technique is a method for bringing to bear at strategic times the residue of the relearning that took place throughout the therapeutic sessions. This relearning, of course, was not limited to the sessions with me. Each success he experienced in managing his anxiety, when interpreted by him as breaking a maladaptive associative bond or connection, constituted a relearning experience. This learning was retrieved and brought to bear on managing new anxiety situations in the form of cognitive restructuring in a kind of positive feedback system to counteract the negative feedback system that had become a stable feature of his cognitive-perceptual system.

Bill took well to cognitive restructuring. He practiced it systematically when he woke up in the morning, often with anxious thoughts, as well as spontaneously in the course of the day.

As the day for the interview with the regional manager approached, Bill's anxiety increased. I suggested he practice the flooding technique he had learned earlier. He did. The day of the interview came. He was very anxious. He felt a panic driving to the interview; "like I was going to be executed," he said. During the interview itself, however, he relaxed after a few moments and the rest of the half hour was uneventful. He was offered the job and a starting date was set for approximately six weeks later.

During that period Bill's anxiety varied along a wide range of intensity, but what was now clear to me was that it was a downhill process. The anxiety management techniques were not having the enduring effect that was expected. He reported dreams of being pursued because he had murdered someone. He felt, he said, as if he was holding a hand grenade from which the pin had been pulled. He began drinking heavily again. Benson's Relaxation Response, he said, was not enough. The cognitive restructuring seemed hardly worth doing.

It gradually became clearer to me that the approaching starting date for the new job was not the main generating source of the anxiety that was now engulfing him. It merely provided the context for a counterforce to his moving out that his mother, first subtly but now obviously, had presented. I had underestimated this effect and so had also not seen until now that Bill, indeed, was not in a position, "developmentally" if you will, to take on the responsibilities that a job like this would demand of him. He was overreaching because earlier individuation steps, or stages of separation from his mother, would have to be traversed before this move could be successfully undertaken.

Bill's mother announced a week before he was to start his new job that she decided to leave town for a two-week vacation with a friend. His general anxiety level increased markedly. He got a call a few days before from the regional office asking him whether he would be willing to relocate to another part of the country should this be necessary. He now found that he was anxious all the time. None of the behavioral techniques worked, he said. He drank more.

He appeared on the first day of work and managed somehow to get through it. I saw him three times that week. He felt better after each session, but his high anxiety level was not appreciably reduced. He lasted another week on the job. His mother hadn't returned yet. The following week I received a call from her. Her son, she said, was hospitalized for an acute intestinal problem complicated by excessive drinking. He remained in the general hospital for three days and returned home to recuperate for an additional ten days. When he came for his next session he was haggard and worn.

He told me that he had reached the point where he was drinking all day in order to block out his anxiety. When his mother had returned from her trip he threw himself into her arms and cried. She encouraged him not to return to work. She was, he said, devastated by his overdrinking because it brought back memories of her husband's alcoholism.

Bill subsequently called his employer to say he had to take an indefinite leave of absence because of illness. After being discharged from the hospital he spent his time at home with his mother. He felt more helpless and more powerless than ever before in his life. Whenever he thought of finding employment of any kind, he became anxious. In fact, during his second week after his discharge from the hospital he only left his house to meet his appointments with me. I saw him twice a week for the next four weeks.

My immediate goal became that of helping him to reduce his feelings of helplessness. My support took the form of listening, empathizing, and providing him with alternative cognitive modes of processing his subjective feelings of being overwhelmed. I did this through behavioral concepts such as "learned helplessness." We are all capable of regressing to the point where we believe we cannot do anything. This is how a child feels when faced with the overpowering control of a parent. It is possible, therefore, to unlearn these feelings since they do not correspond to the reality problems we face as adults. Problems have solutions, and we can learn to find them.

I made these cognitive inputs by citing examples of the helplessness other of my patients have felt. This is a common human experience. I followed these cognitive inputs by suggesting a solution to his immediate problem of employment. He looked surprised when I suggested that he return to work at his uncle's restaurant. "Wasn't the whole idea to move away from the protective environment of this family business?" he wondered out loud.

I shared with him the strategy that I had worked out. Moving back into a Greek environment, I reasoned, was a kind of behavioral counterpart to the psychoanalytic concept of "regression in the service of the ego." Bill could be expected to relax in this environment and to be strengthened by the unconditional reinforcement, i.e., support, that he could expect to receive from his uncle and his coworkers at the restaurant. He had often expressed to me the notion that in non-Greek working situations people were highly competitive and would just as soon "chew you up and spit you out." In other words, he experienced the competitiveness of coworkers as inimical and as a personal threat. He experienced the "American" work situation this way because he was socialized in a subculture where mutual support and caring are highly valued behaviors. One is first judged by who one "is," and secondly by what one does. Bill also needed to feel effective at this point; he needed to engage in work he knew how to do and that would produce a steady rate of reinforcements in the form of approval and satisfaction. I envisioned as a next step his procurement of employment in the broader "American" marketplace. He obviously was not ready for this at the time. He also needed to be helped to separate himself emotionally and in a graduated way from the symbiotic relationship he had with his mother. This process would include his learning to relate in more adult ways to women. This whole thrust in the treatment needed to be undertaken gradually, however, as Bill became stabilized emotionally by engaging in a work environment where the probability of success was high and where he could be sure to be accepted and supported.

THE NEXT SIX MONTHS OF TREATMENT

The strategy outlined above was remarkably effective in meeting the planned therapeutic objectives. During the next six months I saw Bill on a once-a-week basis and he stabilized emotionally. The anticipated effects of the work environment he was in were realized. His anxiety was brought under control, his depression lifted, and his self-esteem was restored.

When Bill had announced to his mother that he was going back to work at his uncle's restaurant, she expressed disappointment. She had hoped, she said, that he would accomplish more in life than being a waiter. He was feeling more angry at her now than he could ever remember feeling before; he could almost believe, he said, that she didn't want him to get better. He related to me a repetitive dream he had of his mother dying. He took up with me his reactivated doubts about going to work at the restaurant; I reminded him that this was a transitional step and he could later move in other directions when it became clearer what he wanted to do.

The work situation over the next six months provided Bill with the opportunity to make gains in two important areas. The first was his anxiety about being judged by authority figures; the second was his anxiety about exerting his authority over subordinates. These were obviously two aspects of the same issue.

He identified his anger and the anxiety it activated when his uncle treated him arbitrarily. Bill was not "Greek" enough to be able to accept his uncle's ascribed prerogative to be dominant over those below him in the restaurant hierarchy, and he also was not "American" enough to be able to assert his rights as an individual in a democratic system. His confusion left him feeling helpless and enraged. I made the above cultural distinction for him, and then in the office we rehearsed ways that he could assert himself with his uncle without violating the uncle's dignity as the dominant "boss." Essentially, Bill stood up to him, asserting his position in a forceful manner, while at the same time openly expressing his respect. He tactfully chose appropriate times to do this when other workers were not around. His uncle got the message and began to treat Bill with more respect. He assigned him greater responsibilities in managing the large number of waiters and waitresses.

The behavioral rehearsal we did in relation to his uncle generalized to the interactions he had as the maître d responsible for the work of the staff of waiters and waitresses. They gradually began to treat him with more respect after he successfully handled two or three incidents when waiters had initially refused to conform with the work schedules that he had set up. They challenged his authority, but he stood his ground firmly and without anger and they conformed. These experiences served to reinforce Bill's sense of control over his environment in pervasive ways.

He now began to stand up more to his mother. He refused to tell her of his whereabouts when he stayed out late. He was not as available to her at home to do chores. She began to develop psychosomatic complaints. Her head hurt, her stomach hurt.

What was especially upsetting to her were the changes in Bill's daily routine that progressively decreased the amount of time he spent at home. Since he began work in the late afternoon or early evening he customarily spent the major portion of the day, after arising late in the morning, at home. Now he left the house shortly after he got up and often went to work without returning home. This was a consequence of the lifestyle restructuring we were working on in the therapeutic sessions.

It had become clearer to me after Bill started working again at his uncle's restaurant that his lifetyle was, in general, an impoverished one. He essentially worked from late afternoon until early morning, slept until mid-morning, and then spent the intervening leisure time reading books in his room or interacting with his mother, usually about chores that needed to be done. He saw his girl friend on his day off, and occasionally stayed overnight at her apartment. They sometimes went to a show together. He continued to make very little of this relationship in the sessions with me. I decided to wait before focusing on it until I felt he was well stabilized himself. At this point, I wanted to help him expand the range of reinforcers, i.e., gratifications, he received during his leisure time.

I introduced what was a new and perplexing concept for Bill—that gratifications were an important ingredient of mental health. It was crucial for him at this time to explore ways in which he could increase the frequency of experiences outside of work that produced pleasure. I specified that I was not referring to sensual pleasure as such, but rather to the broader range of interactions with his environment that resulted in a sense of well-being. Usually these involved interactions in which he could feel effective.

It was not easy to get this concept across. Bill's notion of pleasure based on Greek value orientations was clearly a "being" one. One got pleasure exclusively by resting physically, by being nourished through food and drink, and being satisfied sexually by a woman. The more American "doing" orientation as a source of pleasure was foreign to him. He engaged in sports only rarely and had few interests outside of working, except for reading.

I asked him first to monitor his daily activities for a week. He was surprised at how little he did outside of work and being with his mother. We reviewed the full range of alternative possibilities. I actually programmed an alternative lifestyle with him. He started jogging daily after getting up. He registered for accounting courses at a college, since he considered this might be helpful for the career he would later pursue. He contacted some male friends he hadn't seen for awhile and arranged to play softball on Saturday mornings. He developed a latent interest in fishing.

This lifestyle restructuring effort was accomplished over several weeks. He felt markedly better; his anxiety level decreased. This effort also brought into sharper relief for him his dependency on his mother. He was, of course, always aware of it, but now his own collusion in his dependency interactions became more apparent to him. As he moved away from her she intensified her efforts to draw him back. He was better able to handle his own anxiety about this progressive separation from her because of the reinforcing consequences of his new lifestyle. He felt strong now because his independence from her was associated with the increase of daily reinforcements. Bill's Americanization was also, in effect, his course for individuation.

He also transferred a good deal of his dependent needs to me. I shall deal later with how this transference problem was handled. At this point, let me say that he separated from me in the end in the same way that he was doing now from his mother, by effectively interacting with the environment in a direction that assured the appropriate means of gratifying his needs for intimacy. Bill also became aware, as he moved away from his mother, of her irrational fears. Her experience with the world as being unmanageable and always threatening to overwhelm her was, he could now see, mirrored in his own perceptions and cognitions. He could observe himself making self-statements that reflected her feelings of helplessness and vulnerability. He could now interrupt these self-statements more easily with more rational ones in his cognitive restructuring effort.

Bill continued to do Benson's Relaxation Response twice a day during this period. He also did the flooding technique whenever he was unable to handle through appropriate actions an anxiety-evoking interaction with his mother, his boss, or his coworkers. He now did the flooding at home without my necessarily assigning it. He was fully inducted by now into the concept of desensitization as a paradigm for managing anxiety in its various forms. He knew that Benson's Relaxation Response, cognitive restructuring, graduated approaches to real life situations, and assertion training all incorporated the same principle of immunization through progressive exposure to anxiety-evoking events. Bill had learned how to manage stress.

It was now about a year after my initial contact with him. He was stabilized; his anxiety was for the first time under control. The therapeutic alliance with me was consolidated. However, in the two major spheres of life, love and work, a great deal remained to be done.

THE FINAL PHASE OF TREATMENT: THE NEXT 16 MONTHS

I saw Bill on a once-a-week basis over the next nine months and then once a month, in the final termination phase, for seven months. He made rapid progress in the two spheres of love and work. The therapeutic sessions were used to plan the directions he would move from week to week, and the specific steps he would take. I monitored his progress with him. I contracted with him to make specific moves when his resistance hampered him. I suggested different techniques to use to manage his anxiety when he confronted anxiety-evoking events. I reinforced him continually for his successes and taught him to accept his failures. He regressed from time to time and, in fact, reverted to overdrinking on at least three occasions, although only for short periods. I provided informational inputs; that is, I helped him broaden his understanding of such life events as man-woman relationships and relationships among people in organizational settings. In the end we dealt with his transference feelings to me. At the end of this final phase of treatment, Bill was ensconced in a satisfying job and was preparing to get married.

In the remainder of this chapter I will describe in narrative form the major features of Bill's successful struggle to individuate in the areas of love and work.

He was prepared now to make specific moves in these two directions. We reviewed various strategies together. Initially, I thought it would be an important next step for him to move out of his mother's house and into an apartment. He resisted this. I pushed a little. It finally became clear that, in fact, this was still too large a step. The thought alone made him too anxious. He needed a bridging relationship with a woman, I thought, before he could effectively separate from his mother emotionally. He agreed. The relationship with Connie was satisfying, but he always thought of it as a transitory affair. In fact, it was regressive because she provided a great deal of nurturance for him and he gave very little back. She made few demands. He didn't value her as an emotional equal. He was not yet capable of nurturing another person or of investing in, and loving, a woman.

I suggested he broaden his experience with women by dating more. He shared his concerns that by doing so he would put himself in the position of being rejected. He also shared his belief that success with a woman meant getting her to bed on the first date and "scoring." He was relieved to learn that this was a limited perspective not shared by most men. This "macho" concept included the belief that once he got a woman into bed she was no longer to be valued because she was a sexually loose woman. Concurrently, he subscribed to the belief that women were equal to men and so had the same rights in the sexual sphere as men. I asked him how he reconciled these discrepant views. He looked confused. He wasn't aware until now of this inconsistency in his thinking. I thought to myself that this was another instance of cultural value orientation discrepancy. The rural Greek values of his parents had not given way to those of the current American society in which he lived. He offered the additional view that non-Greek girls were fair game, while Greek girls were to be respected.

He started dating other women without letting Connie know. He started to see a Greek-American woman, Dianne, who was waitressing at his uncle's restaurant. He began seeing her regularly. He was getting attached to her and this stimulated his anxiety. His worry was that she might abandon him. He decided to make her fall in love with him to assure himself that she would not leave. He worked on it, and was able to say that he wanted her to become dependent on him like Connie was. He didn't sleep with her at first. He reported having disturbing dreams. He couldn't remember the content in the morning but he woke up feeling anxious. Then he remembered parts of one dream in which he was alone in a desert feeling helpless and was unable to find his way home.

His mother approved of this relationship. She involved herself in the whole affair. Bill tried to ward her off, but she managed to get him to tell her how things were progressing.

Bill and I also decided that he should start making corollary moves in the career direction. I contracted with him to start reading want ads again. The thought generated some anxiety, but only of a mild degree. He was almost enthusiastic about the prospect. The Boston Sunday paper ran an ad about a hotel management training program being offered by a major hotel chain. This sounded just right. As the day for the interview with the program directors approached, Bill's anxiety mounted. I suggested that he do the flooding exercise using scenes from his last job situation. He relived the traumatic events of this last abortive job effort. One scene, the most anxiety-evoking one, was the situation where he was asked to stand up before a group of colleagues and review his work progress of the previous work. The other scene was based on an interview he had had with the very authoritarian owners of the company. These scenes still were powerful in their anxiety-evoking potential. Specifically, they generated feelings of being helpless and powerless in the face of being criticized and rejected. He flooded them five to six times a week for two weeks. Each flooding session at home lasted a full 40 minutes.

His interview with the program directors went well. He was accepted into the program. He kept his restaurant job on a part-time basis, continuing to work there three nights a week. It made him feel secure that he had somewhere to return if he failed. Connie provided this function in the love area. In both situations I viewed these maneuvers as pacing his movement outward by taking graduated steps, rather than "burning his bridges" behind him. It was not avoidance, because he was broaching new tasks and new situations.

The training aspect of the program was to take six months. It involved role playing exercises in which he was required to present before the group of his cotrainees. He was also required to travel around the state and later throughout New England in order to get "hands on" experience. Each one of these tasks generated anxiety, but he successfully managed them. He had some trying moments and crises, but he confronted them and coped effectively in the end.

His relationship with Dianne went through various phases. He became sexually involved with her, broke off with Connie, and thought about getting married. Dianne was "hooked" and wanted to set the date. Bill began feeling entrapped by her and had second thoughts. This was followed by a period of intense jealousy. He now became aware, in ways he was not aware of before, that she was very seductive with other men. He complained; she reassured him, but when he kept avoiding the topic of marriage she became openly flirtatious with other men and related affairs she had had in the past (one with a married man who was an acquaintance of Bill's). His jealousy reached paranoid proportions. He only felt safe with her when they were having sex. Afterwards his suspicions of who she might be with when he was not around returned. He was obsessed with the issue of her fidelity. He remembered bits and pieces of disturbing dreams. Always they included the theme of being abandoned by a woman who ran off with another man. I interpreted his "Oedipal" theme as reflecting his early attachment to his mother. It didn't help much. What did help was the flooding technique. We constructed a series of scenes in which Dianne was engaged in a variety of sexual acts with other men. His anxiety reached 90 s.u.d.s. We did the flooding in the office, spending most of the 50 minutes on it for four consecutive weeks. He did it twice a day at home for 30 to 40 minute periods before doing Benson's Relaxation Response. It finally worked; he no longer was anxious about her and his paranoid feelings disappeared. He began now to feel anger at her for pressing him about marriage and he confronted her with this feeling. He was no longer worried that she would abandon him. He also confronted his mother, expressing his outrage at her for her intrusion into his life. He did this in a controlled and effective manner. Her psychosomatic symptoms increased. He was not intimidated. She totaled her car one night and narrowly escaped serious injury. He regressed a bit, felt guilty and blamed himself and me, but then recovered quickly and could take a more realistic view of the events.

He took up with his brother and sister the issue of sharing responsibility for their mother. They were sympathetic and cooperative and explained that she refused invitations to come out West even for brief visits. Bill was more affirmative now about this issue with his mother. She abruptly decided to visit his sister for a month. He had a momentary pang of fear at her leaving, but overcame this quickly.

When she returned he announced that he was moving into an apartment of his own. Surprisingly, his mother, when she realized that he meant it, quickly became reconciled to the idea.

Bill reevaluated his relationship with Dianne and decided she was not the woman he wanted to be with. She had already sensed this and didn't "go crazy" when he told her he was not going to marry her. He called up Connie who refused to see him. She had not yet recovered from his rejection of her and was still furious at him. He persevered. She reluctantly agreed to date him. She was very cautious. Bill could now invest in her in ways he never could before. He felt warm, tender, nurturing feelings for her. When he finished the hotel management training program and was assigned to a large hotel in another part of the state, he asked Connie to marry him.

I saw Bill on a once-a-month basis in the six-month period prior to his marriage. This was a protracted termination phase. It was not a very emotional separation period. He was now fully invested in Connie and enjoying his job. In both spheres he was "reinforced" in that he felt effective and loved. He clearly didn't need me anymore, nor did he express much anxiety at the prospect of separating from me. It was happening in a gradual way and he felt no need to verbalize his feelings about me. I understood that he felt strong positive feelings toward me of the kind that Greek men do not express directly to each other. He could now be a father in his own house.

9
Summary

In summary, some additional theoretical considerations will be reviewed. The principles outlined in Chapter 4, Clinical Issues, were elucidated in the analysis of the therapeutic process described in the four case histories that were presented. These cases were selected in order to demonstrate how the interrelationship between the focal symptom and the total functioning of the individual is conceptualized theoretically and dealt with therapeutically. These were individuals in whom the delimiting effect of their symptoms reflected a truncated lifestyle.

These cases are not atypical of those seen in general psychotherapy cases. Experienced therapists of different theoretical persuasions will quickly identify in their treatment of patients many of the therapeutic processes that are described here as similar to those in which they are engaged. These commonalities, although certainly real, may serve, however, to obscure the idiosyncratic nature of the behavioral approach presented in this book.

The complexity of the neurotic patterns in these patients mitigated against the so-called classical behavioral approach, in which the behavioral analysis leads to identification of relevant "target" behaviors that are then modified by the application of appropriate techniques. This would indeed have been a simplistic and certainly ineffective tactic. It became necessary, instead, to order the interaction of intricately connected historical, situational, and future events in the life of the patient and the disordered thinking, feeling, and acting that characterized their behavior in the present. It was through confronting relevant present events in the life of the patient that changes took place, and not through insight into unresolved conflicts in the past. These changes, furthermore, were experienced as enhanced, effective interactions with the environment. And they were observable, demonstrable, palpable changes. Bill Anastos was able to manage his separation anxiety; he was thereby liberated to learn to invest emotionally in a woman, and to perform effectively and

132

responsibly in a job commensurate with his abilities. Millie Collingsworth was able to overcome her contamination phobia and then to confront her inhibitions in the sexual area. Paul Cohen was able to diminish significantly his obsessive-compulsive ruminative behavior. The reduction of his catastrophic fears allowed him to separate emotionally from his parents and to develop a satisfying relationship with a woman. He was also able to pass his exams. Mrs. Wilson not only overcame her phobias, she also learned, as part of this therapeutic process, to assert her legitimate needs with her husband. The elimination of the presenting symptoms in these four patients became part of a broader individuation process that resulted in significant lifestyle changes.

These changes were guided in each step of the therapy by the application of learning theory principles, both respondent and operant. The therapy required, also, replicative and instigative functions of the therapist. The 50-minute-hour was employed in deconditioning specific maladaptive cognitive and affective reactions by simulating, i.e., replicating, the individual's interactions with the relevant conditions in his/her world. The appropriate techniques were systematic desensitization in the case of Mrs. Wilson's phobias, flooding in the case of Bill Anastos's "Oedipal" fears, and cognitive restructuring in the case of Paul Cohen's obsessive-ruminative behaviors. These replicative functions, however, were designed to enhance the actual confrontation of those situations that were being avoided in the real world. In this sense, then, they are not corollary to the free associative process in orthodox psychoanalysis or the consciousness-raising process in Gestalt therapy. The behavior therapist instead employs his techniques to facilitate his instigative efforts with his patient. Through contracting and other directive means the therapist arranged for the patient to actually engage in the previously avoided behaviors. Mrs. Collingsworth was instructed not to decontaminate when she felt the urge to do so in order to relieve anxiety. Bill Anastos was contracted to date women and to look for a job. Paul Cohen moved into an apartment of his own.

The therapeutic alliance provided a means of increasing the probability of change through providing a steady source of reinforcement for the patient. The therapeutic relationship was based on the principle of "conditional" and contrasted to "unconditional personal regard." What is meant here is that the patient was expected to work with the therapist toward changing maladaptive behavior. The fact that I cared about Mrs. Wilson and Paul Cohen was not the crucial variable that contributed to the successful outcome—the reality that I expected each of them to change their behavior is what made it possible for them to do so. This expectation was based on the belief that they were capable of changing. In this sense, the therapeutic alliance was designed to provide an important condition for change.

While the transference was a real part of the relationship with each of these patients, it would be a misperception to conclude that that is where the changes occurred. Feelings toward the therapist originating in the early conditioning history of the patient were indeed generalized to the therapist. They were not, however, focused on and therefore extinguished in an undramatic way. The patients' major energies were directed to modifying his/her reactions to significant interpersonal events in their real world. This is where the corrective experiences occurred, not in intrapsychic reconstructions based on insight. Bill Anastos did not need to "work through" his obvious transference to me. He had learned to manage authority figures effectively in his interactions with his uncle, bosses, and other people.

It becomes evident, based on the above considerations, why modern "ego" oriented psychodynamic approaches should not be equated with the behavioral approach proposed here (Mann, 1973). These short-term psychotherapy approaches differ in that they are based on the principle of intraindividual change through "insight." They indeed focus on the adaptive functions of the "ego" in relation to coping with real life events and so do not exclusively focus on reconstructing past life events. They continue, however, to rely exclusively on intraindividual events, such as cognitive-perceptual and affective processes, and so differ from the behaviorist's focus on individual-environment interactions.

Paradoxically, the modern cognitive-behavior therapy movement also ignores this fundamental difference. Cognitive behavioral theorists, no doubt discouraged by the ineffectiveness of the simplistic version of classical behavior therapeutic approaches to managing complex neurotic disorders, have reversed their theoretical course and have returned to advocating "cognitive restructuring" approaches (Mahoney, 1979). They go beyond the use of cognitive restructuring techniques in managing disordered affect, such as anxiety and depression; such is the case in the behavioral approach described here. They go further and point out that operant theory is based on a behaviorism whose philosophical underpinnings can no longer be defended by modern epistemology (Mahoney, 1977c). While this position cannot be argued here, it can be pointed out that it might be more productive to explore the potential of operant theory in ordering complex clinical phenomena before discarding it for what is essentially an approach based on a different theory and a different philosophy. This book has attempted to further this aim.

References

Adams, H. E., Tollison, C. D., & Carson, T. P. Behavior therapy with sexual deviations. In S. M. Turner, K. S. Calhoun, & H. E. Adams (Eds.), *Handbook of clinical behavior therapy.* New York: John Wiley, 1981.

Azrin, N. H., & Nunn, R. G. Habit reversal: A method of eliminating nervous habits and tics. *Behavior Research and Therapy,* 1973, **11,** 619–628.

Azrin, N. H., Nunn, R. G., & Frantz, S. I. Habit reversal vs. negative practice treatment of nervous tics. *Behavior Therapy,* March 1980, **11**(2), 169–179.

Bandura, A. *Principles of behavior modification.* New York: Holt, Rinehart & Winston, 1969.

Beck, A. *Cognitive therapy and emotion disorders.* New York: International Universities Press, 1976.

Benson, H. *The relaxation response.* New York: Avon Books, 1975.

Blanchard, E. B., Andrasik, F., Ahles, T., Teders, S. J., & O'Keefe, D. Migraine and tension headache: A meta-analytic review. *Behavior Therapy,* November 1980, **11**(5), 613–632.

Bowlby, J. *Separation,* Vol. II. New York: Basic Books, 1973.

Brady, J. P. Metronome-conditioned speech retraining for stuttering. *Behavior Therapy,* 1971, **2.**

Cautela, J. R. Covert sensitization. *Psychological Reports,* 1967, **20,** 459–468.

Cautela, J. R. Behavior therapy and self-control: Techniques and implications. In C. M. Franks (Ed.), *Behavior therapy: Appraisal and status.* New York: McGraw-Hill, 1969.

Cautela, J. R. Covert reinforcement. *Behavior therapy,* 1970, **1,** 33–50.

Cautela, J. R. *Behavior analysis forms for clinical intervention.* Champaign, Ill.: Research Press Co., 1977.

Cautela, J. R., & Bennett, A. K. Covert conditioning. In R. Corsini (Ed.), *Handbook of innovative psychotherapies.* New York: John Wiley, 1981.

Cautela, J. R., & Kastenbaum, R. A. A reinforcement survey schedule for use in therapy, training and research. *Psychological Reports,* 1967, **20,** 1115–30.

Corbett, L. O., & Corbett, N. *Relaxation therapy: An alternative to tension.* Boston, Mass.: Instructional Manual, Film Therapy Associates, 1976.

Davidson, A. M., Denny, D. R., & Elliot, C. H. Suppression and substitution in the treatment of nail-biting. *Behavior Research and Therapy,* 1980, **18,** 1–9.

Diagnostic and Statistical Manual of Mental Disorders. Vol. III. (D.S.M. III) New York: American Psychiatric Association, 1980.

Doleys, D. Behavioral treatments for nocturnal enuresis in children: A review of recent literature. *Psychological Bulletin,* 1977, **84,** 30–54.

Dollard, J., & Miller, N. *Personality psychotherapy.* New York: McGraw-Hill, 1950.

Ellis, A. *Reason and emotion in psychotherapy.* New York: Lyle Stuart, 1962.

Ellis, A. Rational-emotive therapy and cognitive behavior therapy: Similarities and differences. *Cognitive Therapy and Research,* 1980, **7**, 325.

Evans, I. M. (Ed.) *Relaxation techniques: Clinical and training procedures,* Vol. 1. (Cassette Series) New York: Biomonitoring Applications, 1975-1976.

Ferster, C. B. Classification of behavioral pathology. In L. Krasner & L. P. Ullman (Eds.), *Behavior modification: New developments and implications.* New York: Holt, Rinehart and Winston, 1965.

Ferster, C. B. A functional analysis of depression. *American Psychologist,* 1973, **10**(28), 857-870.

Fersterheim, H., & Baer, J. *Don't say yes when you want to say no.* New York: David McKay Co., 1975.

Flowers, J. V. Simulation and role playing methods. In F. H. Kanfer & A. P. Goldstein (Eds.), *Helping people change.* New York: Pergamon Press, 1975.

Goldfried, M. R., & Davison, G. C. *Clinical behavior therapy.* New York: Holt, Rinehart & Winston, 1976.

Greenwood, M. M., & Benson, H. The efficacy of progressive relaxation in systematic desensitization and a proposal for an alternative competitive response—The relaxation response. *Behavior Research and Therapy,* 1977, **15**(4), 337-343.

Hersen, M., & Eisler, R. M. Behavioral approaches to the study and treatment of psychogenic tics. *Genetic Psychology Monographs,* 1973, **87**, 289-312.

Jacobson, E. *Progressive relaxation.* Chicago: University of Chicago Press, 1938.

Kallman, W. M., & Gilmore, J. D. Vascular disorders. In S. M. Turner, K. S. Calhoun, & H. E. Adams (Eds.), *Handbook of clinical behavior therapy.* New York: John Wiley, 1981.

Kanfer, F. H., & Phillips, J. S. A survey of current behavior therapies and a proposal for classification. In C. M. Franks (Ed.), *Behavior therapy: Appraisal and status.* New York: McGraw-Hill, 1969.

Kanfer, F. H., & Saslow, G. Behavioral analysis: An alternative to diagnostic classification. *Archives of General Psychiatry,* 1969, **12**, 529-538. (a)

Kanfer, F. H., & Saslow, G. Behavioral diagnoses. In C. M. Franks (Ed.), *Behavior therapy: Appraisal and status.* New York: McGraw-Hill, 1969. (b)

Krasner, L. Behavior modification—values and training: The perspective of a psychologist. In C. M. Franks (Ed.), *Behavior therapy: Appraisal and status.* New York: McGraw-Hill, 1969.

Lazarus, A. A. *Behavior therapy and beyond.* New York: McGraw-Hill, 1971.

Lewinsohn, P. M. Clinical aspects of depression. In K. S. Calhoun, H. E. Adams, & K. M. Mitchell (Eds.), *Innovative treatment methods of psychopathology.* New York: John Wiley, 1974.

Lewinsohn, P. M., & Graf, M. Pleasant activities and depression. *Journal of Consulting and Clinical Psychology,* 1973, **4**(1), 261-268.

Lewinsohn, P. M., & Libet, J. Pleasant events, activity schedules, and depression. *Journal of Abnormal Psychology,* 1972, **79**, 291-295.

Mahler, M. S., Pine, F., & Bergman, A. *The psychological birth of the human infant.* New York: Basic Books, 1975.

Mahoney, M. *Cognition and behavior modification.* Cambridge, Mass.: Ballinger Publishing Co., 1974.

Mahoney, M. J. Reflections on the cognitive-learning trend in psychotherapy. *American Psychologist,* 1977, **32**, 5.

Mahoney, M. J. Cognitive and non-cognitive views in behavior modification. In P. O. Sjoden & S. Bates (Eds.), *Trends in behavior therapy.* New York: Academic Press, 1979.

Mann, J. *Time limited psychotherapy.* Cambridge: Harvard University Press, 1973.

Marks, I. M. *Fears and phobias.* New York: Academic Press, 1969.

Marks, I. M., Hodgson, R., & Rachman, S. Treatment of chronic-obsessive compulsive neuroses by in vivo exposure. A two-year follow-up and issues in treatment. *British Journal of Psychiatry,* 1975, **127**, 349–364.

Marlatt, G. A., & Perry, M. A. Modeling methods. In F. H. Kanfer & A. P. Goldstein (Eds.), *Helping people change.* New York: Pergamon Press, 1975.

Masters, W. H., & Johnson, V. E. *Human sexual inadequacy.* Boston, Mass.: Little, Brown & Co., 1970.

Meichenbaum, D. *Cognitive-behavior modification.* New York: Plenum Press, 1977.

Melamed, B. G., & Siegel, L. J. Practical application in health care. *Behavioral medicine.* New York: Springer Publishing Co., 1980.

Miller, P. M., & Fox, D. W. Substance abuse. In S. M. Turner, K. S. Calhoun, & H. E. Adams (Eds.), *Handbook of clinical behavior therapy.* New York: John Wiley, 1981.

Mostofsky, D. I. Recurrent paroxysmal disorders of the central nervous system. In S. M. Turner, K. S. Calhoun, & H. E. Adams (Eds.), *Handbook of clinical behavior therapy.* New York: John Wiley, 1981.

Murphy, G. *Historical introduction to modern psychology.* New York: Harcourt, Brace & Co., 1949.

Papajohn, J., & Spiegel, J. *Transactions in families: A modern approach for resolving cultural and generational conflicts.* San Francisco: Jossey-Bass, 1975.

Pavlov, I. P. *[Conditioned reflexes: An investigation of the physiological activity of the cerebral cortex]* (G. V. Anrep, trans.). London: Oxford University Press, 1927.

Pavlov, I. P. *[Conditioned reflexes and psychiatry]* (W. H. Gantt, trans.). New York: International Publishers, 1941.

Poole, A. D., Sauson-Fisher, R. W., & German, G. A. The rapid-smoking technique: Therapeutic effectiveness. *Behavior research and therapy,* Vol. 19, No. 5. New York: Pergamon Press, 1981.

Rachman, S., Hodgson, R., & Marks, I. M. Treatment of chronic oppressive-compulsive neuroses. *Behavior Research and Therapy,* 1971, **9**, 237–247.

Rachman, S., Hodgson, R., & Marks, I. M. Treatment of chronic oppressive-compulsive neuroses: Follow up and further findings. *Behavior Research and Therapy,* 1972, **10**(2), 181–189.

Roper, G., Rachman, S., & Hodgson, R. An experiment on obsessional checking. *Behavior Research and Therapy,* 1973, **11**(3), 271–277.

Rosenbaum, M. S., and Ayllon, T. The habit-reversal technique in treating trichotillomania. *Behavior Therapy,* September 1981, **12**(4), 473–482.

Salter, A. *Conditioned reflex therapy.* New York: Creative Age, 1949.

Sandler, J. Aversion methods. In F. H. Kanfer & A. P. Goldstein (Eds.), *Helping people change.* New York: Pergamon Press, 1975.

Seligman, M. Q. P. *Helplessness.* San Francisco: W. H. Freeman, 1975.

Skinner, B. F. *Science and human behavior.* New York: Macmillan, 1953.

Skinner, B. F. What is psychotic behavior? *Theory and treatment of the psychoses.* Washington University Studies Committee on Publications, Washington University Press, 1956.

Spiegel, J. P. *Transactions: Interplay between the individual, family and society.* J. Papajohn (Ed.) New York: Science House, 1971.

Stampfl, T., & Levis, D. Essentials of implosive therapy: A learning theory based on psychodynamic behavioral therapy. *Journal of Abnormal Psychology,* 1967, **72**, 496–503.

Stuart, R. B. Operant-interpersonal treatment for marital discord. *Journal of Consulting and Clinical Psychology,* 1969, **33**, 675–682.

Sturgis, E. T., & Meyer, V. Obsessive compulsive disorders. In S. M. Turner, K. S. Calhoun, & H. E. Adams (Eds.), *Handbook of clinical behavior therapy.* New York: John Wiley, 1981.

Suinn, R. Rehearsal training for ski racers. *Behavior Therapy,* 1972, **3**, 519–520.

Suinn, R. Anxiety management training for general anxiety. In R. Suinn & R. Weigel (Eds.), *Innovative therapies: Critical and creative contributions.* New York: Harper & Row, 1975.

Twentyman, C. T., & Zimering, R. T. Behavioral training of social skills: A critical review. In
    M. Hersen, R. M. Eisler, & P. M. Miller (Eds.), *Progress in behavior modification,* Vol. 7.
    New York: Academic Press, 1979.
Wachtel, P. L. *Psychoanalysis and behavior therapy: Toward an integration.* New York: Basic
    Books, 1977.
Wolpe, J. Reciprocal inhibition as the main basis of psychotherapeutic effects. *Archives of Neu-
    rology and Psychiatry,* 1954, **72**, 205–226.
Wolpe, J. *Psychotherapy by reciprocal inhibition.* Stanford: Stanford University Press, 1958.
Wolpe, J. Investigating the case: Stimulus-response analysis. In *The practice of behavior thera-
    py.* (2nd ed.) New York: Pergamon Press, 1973.

Author Index

Subject Index

About the Author

John C. Papajohn maintains a private practice in Brookline, Massachusetts. He is co-director of the training program in ethnicity and mental health which is based at Brandeis University. He serves as a consultant in the department of medicine and of psychiatry at the Cambridge City Hospital, Cambridge, Massachusetts. He also is a consultant at the Boston Veterans Administration Hospital, Pilgrim Center in Braintree, Massachusetts and the Hellenic College in Brookline, Massachusetts.

He has previously served as a member of the faculty in the department of Social Relations at Harvard University and the Florence Heller School for Advanced Studies in Social Welfare at Brandeis University.

He has published extensively in the area of culture and mental health and behavior therapy, and is co-author of *Transactions in Families,* a modern approach to resolving cultural and intergenerational problems—Jossey Bass, 1975.

Pergamon General Psychology Series

Editors: Arnold P. Goldstein, Syracuse University
Leonard Krasner, SUNY at Stony Brook